# The Spirit Power

## ~Volume I~

Grace Dola Balogun

"The fruit of the Spirit is

LOVE

JOY

PEACE

LONGSUFFERING

GENTLENESS

GOODNESS

FAITH

MEEKNESS

TEMPERANCE

Against such there is no law."


Galatians 5:22-23

# The Spirit Power
# ~Volume I ~

Grace Dola Balogun

Grace Religious Books
New York, NY

The Spirit Power — Volume I
By Grace Dola Balogun
Copyright © 2012 Grace Dola Balogun
Cover design by Lionsgate Book Design, Lisa Hainline
www.lionsgatebookdesign.com
Interior Design by White Cottage Publishing Company
www.whitecottagepublishing.com

Scripture quotations are from the King James Version of the Holy Bible.

Grace Religious Books Publishing & Distributors books may be ordered through booksellers or by contacting the publisher:

Grace Religious Books Publishing & Distributors, Inc.
213 Bennett Avenue
New York, NY 10040
www.Gracereligiousbookspublishers.com

To contact the author: 1-646-559-2533
info@gracereligiousbookspublishers.com

ISBN: 978-0-9851960-7-8 (epub)
ISBN: 978-0-9851960-8-5 (pdf)
ISBN: 978-0-9851960-6-1 (sc)

Library of Congress Control Number: 2012933498

Printed in the United States of America

*I dedicate this book to the glory of my Lord and Savior Jesus Christ who emptied Himself, came to this earth to save me, a sinner, and blessed me with the salvation of eternal life in Him. May He receive glory, honor, blessings, and power from this book. May He let this book fill the hearts of everyone who reads it with the Spirit Power, now and forever. May Christ indwell, baptize, and fill the hearts of all who read this book with His Spirit. "But ye are not in the flesh, but in the Spirit, if so be that the Spirit of God dwell in you. Now if any man has not the Spirit of Christ, he is none of his." Rom 8:9. This book is from Him to make the power of the Holy Spirit manifest in the lives of all the children of God called by His name: Christians.*

# Contents

# Preface

This Book, *The Spirit Power*, will let you know the power of the Spirit of God as you have never known it before: From the beginning of creation. It will clear away any confusion about the mighty power of the Holy Spirit, the saving Power of the Holy Spirit, and the Power of the fruit of the Holy Spirit that changes the believer's life.

This book will let you know that you need to be filled with the Holy Spirit; you need to be baptized with the Holy Spirit. This book will let you know the power of the indwelling of the Holy Spirit in the lives of believers immediately after conversion.

There is a difference between the indwelling of the Holy Spirit and the baptism of the Holy Spirit. The activities of the Holy Spirit on earth began on the day of the creation of the universe and have continued until the present.

The Holy Spirit is a living being, one of the three members of Godhead. He was active in creation and in sustaining the universe. He conceived Jesus in Mary's womb. He revealed God's will to men and gave the message of salvation. The Spirit also empowered the believers to perform miracles in order to confirm that their message was from God.

The Spirit dwells in the people of God today from the moment of conversion. When they are baptized by immersion, they claim open identification with Christ. If the Spirit of God does not indwell us, we are not a child of God. The Spirit will continue His work until the end of the world.

The Spirit's presence is the fullness of God's presence on earth in the lives of His people, the children of God. The Apostles received Holy Spirit baptism and they were speaking in different languages. It is the same today when we receive the baptism of the Holy spirit and we speaks in tongues and pray with supernatural power.

This book will renew, energize, and awaken your spirit to accept the Spirit's power that will help you to live a holy, healthy, and godly life as a child of God. You will be able to do impossible things that you cannot imagine through the power of the Holy Spirit's supernatural power.

This Book will help you to know that God continues to pour out His Spirit, just as on the day of Pentecost, to those who abide and believe in His Son Jesus Christ our Savior Lord, with obedience to the Word of God in order to receive the gift of eternal life through the power of the Holy Spirit.

*The Spirit Power* is a book that will help you to begin a new life in Christ. Salvation is the gift of Grace with abundant life that the Spirit Power offers. May our Lord and Savior continue to pour out His Spirit on all those who believe in Him.

Prayer: May He let this book bring unbelievers to Christ's feet on the throne of grace. All other religions of the earth will know and worship the true God, the King of kings, the Lord of lords and the God of gods. May every soul of human beings worship, praise, and glorify Him where He sits at the right hand of God the Father.

*The Spirit Power* is an inspirational book and the right book for you. It will lift up your spirit to be in tune with the Spirit of the Almighty God—Father, Son, and Holy Spirit forever one God.

Amen, amen, and amen.

# 1

# The Spirit Power from the Beginning of Creation

The Holy Spirit is the third person of the Trinity. Old Testament believers, such as Moses and all the prophets were saved and sanctified by the Spirit, but not in the same way as New Testament believers the Apostles, people in the early Christianity and up until today because New Testament believers were indwelled with the Holy Spirit.

The Spirit came and went from Old Testament believers like the prophets. He spoke to them and sent them to deliver messages. Old Testament prophets got close to God so that the Spirit of God could use them according to His Will. The signs and symbols of the Holy Spirit in the Old Testament were wind, fire, water, breath, and light.

The role of the Holy Spirit in creation was that God spoke, and the earth was created. The Father spoke, and the earth was created; the Son is the powerful Word through which God created all things. The word became flesh and dwells among us we behold its glory, the glory of the one and only begotten Son of the Father full of Grace and Truth.

"In the beginning was the word, and the word was with God, and the word was God." John 1:1. The scripture plainly tells us why, John calls Christ the Word; the Word is in two folds: Word conceived, and Word uttered. The conceived Word is the thought, which is the first product and conception of the Soul.

Therefore, the second person of the trinity is call the Word; for he is the first begotten of the Father. There is nothing we are surer of then than what we think, nothing we are surer in the dark about than how we think.

So that the generation and births of our eternal mind may well be allowed to be in great mysteries of godliness, the bottom of which we cannot fathom, or comprehend. There is the Word uttered, and this is speech, the chief and most natural indication of the mind.

Christ is the Word, for by him God has in these last days spoken to us. Christ has made known God's mind to us, as a man's word or speech makes known his thoughts. Christ was revealed as the eternal Word of

God. "All things were made by him; and without him was not anything made that was made." John 1:3.

"For by him were all things created, that are in heaven, and that in earth, visible and invisible, whether they be throne, or dominions, or principalities, or powers: all things were created by him, and for him." Col. 1:16.

"God, who at sundry times and in divers manners spake in time past unto the fathers by the prophets, Hath in these last days spoken unto us by His Son, whom he hath appointed heir of all things, by whom also he made the worlds." Heb. 1:1–2.

The Holy Spirit was present and active in the creation of the universe. The Bible states that the Spirit flew over the earth in order to preserve and prepare for God's creative process or activity. The Holy Spirit is the sustainer of the creation; the Spirit of God is the one who has been holding up the earth until today.

If the Spirit of God should leave the earth today, the earth would perish. God created the earth for His glory and honor and He expects glory and honor from all His created beings. God created the universe in order to provide a place for His purpose and plan for humanity to be fulfilled.

God created Adam and Eve in His own image and made them a spirit being so that they could worship, enjoy fellowship, and communicate with

Him in the beauty of His holiness. "God is a Spirit: they that worship Him must worship Him in Spirit and in Truth." John 4:24.

Believers must maintain a personal relationship from this earth to heaven with the Lord. The book of Revelation stated, "And I heard a great voice from heaven saying, Behold, the tabernacle of God is with men, and he will dwell with them, and they shall be his people, and God himself shall be with them, and be their God." Rev. 21:3.

This verse is refers to the New Jerusalem, which is already in existence in heaven and will soon come down to earth as the city of God for which Abraham and all God's faith are waiting, for which God Himself is the architect and builder. The new earth will become God's dwelling place, and He will remain with His people forever.

"The Spirit of God hath made me, and the breath of the Almighty hath given me life." Job 33:4.

"And the earth was without form, and void. And darkness was upon the face of the deep. And the spirit of God moved upon the face of the waters." Gen. 1:2. "If he set his heart upon man if he gathers unto himself his Spirit and his breath." Job 34:14.

"And the Lord said, my spirit shall not always strive with man, for that he also is flesh: yet his days shall be an hundred and twenty years." Gen. 6:3.

The Holy Spirit is the messenger of revelation to humankind, "And Pharaoh said unto his servants, can we find such a one as this is, and a man in whom the Spirit of God is?" Gen. 41:38.

"And I will come down and talk with thee there: and I will take of the Spirit which is upon thee, and will put it upon them; and they shall bear the burden of the people with thee, that thou bear it not thyself alone." Num. 11:17.

The Spirit of God came upon the people in the Old Testament for the purpose of revelation, not for endorsement as a prophet. God will not use those who are not in a proper relationship with him to accomplish His purpose.

The Holy Spirit empowers and enables the people in the Old Testament to build the tabernacle, "And Joshua the son of Nun was full of the Spirit of wisdom; for Moses had laid his hands upon him: and the children of Israel hearkened unto him, and did as the Lord commanded Moses." Deut. 34:9. The Spirit of God selected the leaders of God's people and empowered them to do the work He assigned to them.

The important and valuable desire of all Christians is to know God and experience a close relationship and fellowship with Him. As the children of God, we have the privilege of going to Him through the power of His Spirit that He gave to us. "And I have filled him with the Spirit of God, in wisdom, and in all manner of workmanship." Exo. 31:3.

The spirit of God filled the people of Israel with spiritual equipment and enabled them to carry out a special service to God and to be able to teach others. Believers should pray that the Spirit will bless them with wisdom and know-ledge for the physical skills, medical technological advancement, research, and knowledge that will help people find the cure for all of the deadly diseases that plague the people in the world—a spiritual gift to fulfill God's will for their lives.

The Israelites were able to build the tabernacle and houses and to find medicine to cure sickness. "And he hath filled him with the spirit of God, in wisdom, in understanding, and in knowledge, and in all manner of workmanship." Exo. 35:31.

The Spirit of God comes upon individuals with energizing power, temporarily equipping leaders for physical and military service.

The Holy Spirit supernatural power is combined with inspirational knowledge of prophecy. The Spirit inspires and empowers prophets, sending them to deliver messages to the people of

Israel, guiding them where and how to proclaim the message of God's salvation and judgment.

The Spirit was active in the writing of all the Psalms in the Bible. The writing of Psalms, such as those written by the prophet Isaiah, disclosed the coming of the Messiah as the Spirit revealed it to him. Isaiah develops this in many of his writings: that a new Spirit of judgment and fire will appear.

"When the Lord shall have washed away the filth of the daughters of Zion, and shall have purged the blood of Jerusalem from the midst thereof by the Spirit of judgment, and by the spirit of burning." Isa. 4:4.

Believers will be separated from the sinful universe, cleansed from all defilement by Christ's blood and regenerated by the Holy Spirit over them, which will fly with the glory of God like a canopy.

Isaiah's prophecy is that the Spirit of God will empower the Messiah with wisdom, power, knowledge, and holiness. He will be poured out corporately on all of God's people to bring about justice, righteousness, and peace for all of the people of the earth forever.

We have to consider Prophet Ezekiel's prophecy through the power of the Holy Spirit. He experienced the Spirit power when the Spirit sometimes lifted him up from prostration and often transported him to a new location. God promised to give him a new Spirit, a new heart, and a new name.

He said, "And I will put my Spirit within you, and cause you to walk in my statues, and ye shall keep my judgments, and do them. A new heart also will I give you, and a new Spirit will I put within you: and I will take away the stony heart out of your flesh, and I will give you an heart of flesh." Eze. 36:26–27.

God promised to renew the children of Israel physically and spiritually, which required giving them a new heart that was gentle, so that they would be able to respond to God's Word. God's will imparted His Spirit on them, which continued with New Testament believers.

Without the indwelling Spirit, it is impossible to live a true Christian life and to be obedient to God's commandments and God's will. It is very important for all believers to maintain a close relationship with the Lord so that the Holy Spirit may continue to guide, control, and direct the believer according to the will of God. God sent His new Spirit to the Israelites to move them to obey the law and receive the fulfillment of His promises.

Prophet Joel's prophecy was "And it shall come to pass afterwards that I will pour out my

Spirit upon all flesh, and your sons and daughter shall prophecy, your old men shall dream dreams, your young men hall see visions, And also upon the servants, and upon the handmaids in those days will I pour out my spirit." Joel 2:28–32. Apostle Peter quoted this verse on the day of Pentecost when the prophecy was fulfilled.

Prophet Joel's prophecy was that, through the Spirit of God, God would pour out His Spirit on everyone who calls on His Holy Name. This outpouring results in the flowing of the Spirit's manifestation among the people of God. Peter explained the outpouring of the Spirit on those who believe in Jesus Christ and become baptized.

These promises to all those who accept Christ as Lord allow believers to be filled with the Holy Spirit's Power. God spoke through the prophet Joel many years before it would happen. Joel envisions that, one day, the outpouring of the Spirit will be the impartation of the Spirit of God as a gift from God.

The manifestation of the Spirit through His gifts makes visible God's presence among His people. God pours out His Spirit, on the day of Pentecost, on individuals regardless of whether they are a man or woman, whether they are old or young, and regardless of their social status or ethnicity, according to His good pleasure.

Also, other prophets, like Micah, Haggai, and Zachariah, all confirm the Spirit's Power in their lives; they all connect the activities of its presence with their empowerment for building and rebuilding the temple the Spirit of God gives orders, commands, and directions and the people of God follow.

The same Spirit of God that became active in the creation during Old Testament times is still active in the New Testament and will continue until Christ returns. Our Lord's earthly ministry was Spirit-led; there are many significant manifestations of this, including the fulfillment of prophecy.

"The Spirit of the Lord God is upon me; because the Lord hath anointed me to preach good tidings unto the meek; he hath sent me to bind up the brokenhearted, to proclaim liberty to the captives, and the opening of the prison to them that are bound." Isa. 61:1.

The miracles of our Lord were the activities of the Holy Spirit. Jesus Christ's signs and wonders directly revealed God's Spirit at work upon or on Him. As the Spirit empowered Jesus, Jesus promises believers the Holy Spirit that the Spirit will, in the same way, empower His believers to do the work of God.

The Spirit is the helper who will remain in us forever. The Spirit will equip and enable believers to be able to serve the Lord, boldly do the work of the Gospel, and confidently proclaim the Word of God. Believers will be constantly filled with the Spirit so that they will be able to courageously speak and preach for Christ.

The Spirit is God's agent for bringing people to himself and helping them to mature spiritually; only through His power will individuals first receive God's Word as the divine Word.

The Spirit makes unique spiritual insights available to all believers through the use of the Word of God, which makes believers obedient to God and stand on the truth of the Word of God, which many unbelievers cannot do.

The Spirit of God helps believers in prayers, helping them to maintain an intimate relationship with God. God had a plan from the beginning of Creation and He is the only one who can carry it out, at His own time.

Christ will come back to earth, according to God's plan. When that time comes, God will speak and Christ will return to earth. God is a trinity called the Holy Trinity Father,

Son, and Holy Spirit. The Word of God means Elohim this name is used whenever the power of God is revealed, the Bible tells us that Godhead was involved in the creation and also tell us what each of Godhead's activities during the creation were. God created the earth. The Spirit of God is moving and vibrating with supernatural energy; the Holy Spirit brought energy into the formless, void, and dark earth.

The Holy Spirit poured out energy into the universe, God called light into existence, and this light was the result of the outpouring of energy that the Holy Spirit had pumped into the earth. The Spirit power illuminated the universe and dissolved the dark and void earth.

God the Father spoke and everything was created and He pronounced them good. Sin filled the earth, the Spirit of God spoke again, and His word became flesh and dwelled among us. When God spoke, the Son acted; Jesus, the Son of God, is the creator.

"Who is the image of the invisible God, first born of every creature: For by Him were all things created, that are in heaven, and that are in earth, visible, invisible, whether they be thrones, or dominions, or principalities, or powers: all things were created by him, and for him." Col. 1:15-16.

Our Lord said, "But the hour cometh and now is, when true worshipers shall worship the Father in Spirit and in Truth: for the Father seeketh such to worship Him. God is a Spirit: and they that worship Him must worship Him in Spirit and in truth." John 4:23-24.

Jesus Christ is the creator and the sustainer of all things. The Father spoke, the Son carried out the order, and the Spirit enabled believers to respond to the command of God. "God, who at sundry times and in divers manners spake in time past unto the fathers by the prophets hath in these last days spoken unto us by his son, whom he hath appointed heir of all things, by whom also he made the world." Heb. 1:1-2.

God the Father made the world through the operation of Jesus Christ His son, which brings us back to the beginning of creation, which shows that Jesus is the Word of God. God spoke and Christ came into being; the Holy Spirit put Christ in Mary's womb and sustained Him with Hid power until His birth, throughout His ministry and work, and until the day of His resurrection and ascension when the Spirit took Christ back to heaven.

Our Lord said to Philip: "If ye had known me, ye should have known my Father also: and from henceforth ye know him, and have seen Him. Philip said unto Him, Lord shew us the Father, and it sufficeth us. Jesus said unto him, have I been so long time with you, and yet hast thou not known me, Philip? He that hath seen me hath seen the Father, and how sayest thou then, show us the Father? Believest thou not that I am in the Father, and the Father in me? The words that I speak unto you I speak not of myself: but the Father that dwelleth in me, he doeth the works." John 14:7-9.

Jesus Christ is the Spirit of God; He is the Word of God and the Word of God is God. Our Lord said, "I am the true vine, and my Father is the husbandman, every branch that beareth fruit, He purgeth it, that it may bring forth more fruits." John 15:1-2.

These verses of Scripture indicate that the Holy Trinity, the Godhead, is one that it worked together in the creation and continues to sustain the earth. Jesus is the source of life and the Holy Spirit produces fruit.

God the Father, through the power of the Spirit, washes us clean so that we can bear more fruits. The Father also separates the branches if they are withered and dry. We must realize that each member of the Godhead operates together in unity in bringing about and sustaining the creation.

Elohim means more than one name, it means that God is great and that His greatness is in His power, in His strength, and in His might; God's greatness is clearly seen in all that He has created, especially in his actions towards His people, the children of God. God was the Son on earth doing everything through Him.

He exhibited His greatness by forgiving our sins through our Lord Jesus Christ and showing us His infinite love, loving kindness, mercy, and goodness through His Son. God's greatness is unsearchable, unattainable, incomparable, and indescribable.

After the Spirit of God energized the earth, God said let there be light and light came upon the earth. God placed the light permanently in heaven; God is the light-bearer and the light of the world. The primary purpose of the light activity of the Holy Spirit was to create signs for marking the seasons, days, nights, and years.

The light of God in the universe is one of the most powerful activities of the Spirit of God. All Christians experience the light of the Holy Spirit in their heart. If the Spirit illuminates the heart, that heart will never be the same.

When God said, "Let us make a man in our image." God was referring to the Holy Trinity. The Spirit power is dynamic and powerful; through Him, God brings creation into existence and reaches the goal of the new creation in Jesus Christ.

If the Father functions as the source of being and the Son bears witness of God into the world, the Spirit's function has been to complete the task of creation so that the community of the triune

God may come into the fullness. The Spirit of God continues to renew the face of the earth and He will continue until the end. God's Spirit breathed into Adam and he became a living soul,

"And the Lord God formed man of the dust of the ground, and breathed into his nostrils the breath of life, and man became a living soul." Gen.2:7. "Thou sendest forth thy Spirit, they are created: and thou renewest the face of the earth." Psl.104:30.

"The Spirit of God hath made me, and the breath of the Almighty had given me life." Job 33:4. The psalmist is saying, Lord God of creation you created all things and you care for all thy creations. You, O Lord, sustained the earth with thy Spirit because you dwell in the world with your providence and sustain the universe. Your involvement and your work of redemption reflect thy glory.

The Spirit is a life-giver, giving life to those who are spiritually dead and making them alive in Him. The Spirit is the source of life in the universe; the Spirit awakens human life; in beauty and truth, the Spirit of God is present.

The Holy Spirit leads us to experience God in life and the Spirit sheds light on all mysteries when we see the Spirit as the Lord and giver of life, making what we thought was impossible,

possible, and helping us to focus on the divine mystery of the gift of grace and renewed life. The Spirit of God's presence in the world helps us to get closer to the only God, in whom we move, live, and exist, who is not far from us, and who is present with us in all of our earthly problems.

We are able to approach God in times of sadness, joy, hope, suffering, and struggle, and when faced with all other adversities in the world. The Spirit not only formed and shaped our habitable space, but it has also grieved the violence committed against what has been created.

The Spirit is the source of transient life and also of the eternal life of all believers. The Spirit is the Spirit of preservation, preserving and sustaining the universe, as well as preparing the universe for new creation.

The Holy Spirit is active in all corners of creation, moment by moment, in the history of the world. The Spirit of God is present and active in the entire history of salvation. The purpose and goal of creation is for the Spirit of God to unite all things through Christ and for Christ. "Hear, O Israel: The Lord our God is one Lord." Deut. 6:4.

The Bible refers to God as the Father, the Son, and the Holy Spirit. One of the greatest mysteries of God is that He is a triune God; yet, He is one. We have knowledge that the three parts of the Godhead are one; but God works in different ways.

In order to understand the fruit of the Spirit, we must, first of all, understand who the Spirit is, what the Spirit does to help us in our lives, and how He helps us to live a life that will glorify the Lord. The Holy Spirit is the third person of the Godhead, the triune God.

God lives and dwells in our heart in the form of the Holy Spirit; He comes to live inside believers. The Holy Spirit's other names are the Helper, *Paraclete*, and the Invisible Power of God. "In whom ye also trusted, after that ye heard the word of truth, the Gospel of your salvation: in whom also after that ye believed, ye were sealed with that Holy Spirit of promise, which is the earnest of our inheritance until the redemption of the purchased possession, unto the praise of His glory." Eph. 1:13-14.

The Holy Spirit is a deposit, like a first installment of a down payment, guaranteeing our inheritance and given to all believers as a down payment for what we are going to have in full in the future. The Holy Spirit's presence and work in the lives of all Christians pledges our future inheritance.

The Scriptures clarify where the Holy Spirit comes from and what the Spirit's responsibilities in the lives of believers are. "And I will pray the

Father, and He shall give you another Comforter, that he may abide with you forever." John 14:16.

Jesus said that He would ask the Father to give comfort to only those who are serious about their love for Him and their devotion to His Word. Jesus made this statement to let us know how important our continuing love and obedience to God's Word is. "But the Comforter, the Holy Ghost, whom the Father will send in my name, he shall teach you all things, and bring all things to your remembrance, whatsoever I have said unto you." John 14:26.

The most important thing about the Holy Spirit is that He is Holy, and He wants all Christians to acquire His holy character in their lives. The Holy Spirit, according to the Scriptures, was sent by God the Father, to teach believers all things and to bring all of the things that God has said into the believers' remembrance. "And when he is come, he will reprove the world of sin, and of righteousness, and of judgment."John 16:8.

The Holy Spirit will convince believers of Christ of what is right and what is wrong, He will guide believers into the truth of the Gospel, and He will speak only the words that he hears from God. He will disclose to the believer what is going to come in the future and, most important, He will glorify the Lord Jesus Christ. The Holy Spirit prays for us the prayer that cannot be uttered, "The Spirit itself beareth witness with our Spirit that we are children of God." Rom. 8:16. All Christians must know that the Holy Spirit imparts the confidence to us that, through Christ and with Christ, we are the children of God.

The Spirit of God made the truth of Jesus Christ clear to us, that Christ loved us and will continue to love us in heaven as our Mediator of a new Covenant. The Holy Spirit created and imparted the love of God in believers' hearts so that we confidently cry out to Him Abba, Father.

Believers have the knowledge that each person has a spirit and that the Holy Spirit speaks to our spirits to remind us that we are the children of God through Jesus Christ's complete work of redemption. "Now he that hath wrought us for the selfsame thing is God, who also hath given unto us the earnest of the Spirit." 2 Cor. 5:5.

God has a purpose for our life. God's Holy Spirit knows what that purpose is and He will guide believers towards that purpose. The Holy Spirit is given as a deposit to every believer who has accepted Jesus Christ as their personal Lord and Savior.

This means that God wants believers to know that they are the children of God and the family of God as joint heirs with Jesus Christ. God the

Father, who is the Godhead, sends the Holy Spirit; His Spirit lives in believers at the time of conversion and salvation. "In whom ye also trusted, after that ye heard the word of truth, the gospel of your salvation: in whom also after that ye believed, ye were sealed with that Holy Spirit of promise. Which is the earnest of our inheritance until the redemption of the purchased possession, unto the praise of his glory." Eph. 1:13-14.

This verse is telling us that: Heaven is our inheritance. All the blessings that we have in hand are but small if compared with the inheritance. We are sealed with that Holy Spirit of promise. He makes us holy. He is the promised Spirit.

By him believers are sealed and set apart for God. His comforts are earnests of everlasting joys. "If any of you lack wisdom, let him ask of God, that giveth to all men liberally, and upbraideth not; and it shall be given." Jas. 1:5.

We must ask God for wisdom in coping with our trials, not just for deliverance from our troubles; we must ask for wisdom in any decision-making, wisdom about our circumstances, and wisdom and understanding of God's Word and God's will for our lives.

We must ask for wisdom to be able to see this in a spiritual way and to evaluate with our life experience as well as to make the right choices and do the right thing in accordance with God's will revealed in us and with His word and the leadership of the Holy Spirit.

As believers read, study, and meditate on the Word of God, the Holy Spirit helps believers to remember what they have read; in times of need the Spirit will take the word out to comfort the believer and to clear some of the difficulties that the believer might be going through at that particular time.

Believers must read the Word of God daily as food for their soul. "Thy word have I hid in mine heart, that I might not sin against thee." Ps. 119:11. The Holy Spirit convicts believers of sins; the Holy Spirit is the innermost voice that believers hear inside of them, telling them right from wrong.

Believers must be sure that they are listening to the Spirit of God. The way to know the difference is to know God's Word. The way to know God's Word is by reading and studying the Word of God (the Bible) daily.

Reading the Bible will allow believers to grow in their faith and be strengthened this will help them to be able to recognize the voice of the Holy Spirit when He speaks to their hearts, or through Scripture. He guides us into the truth. The truth of the Word of God in the Bible teaches believers the way of God, which is different than the way of the world. "For my thoughts are not your thoughts, neither are your ways my ways, said the Lord. For as the heavens are higher than the earth, so are my ways higher than your ways and my thoughts than your thoughts." Isa. 55:8-9.

The Holy Spirit speaks only the Word of God, which means that believers can be sure that whatever they hear from the Spirit will be consistent with the Word of God. In the Gospel of John, "Howbeit when he, the Spirit of truth, is comes, he will guide you into all truth: for he shall not speak of himself; but whatsoever he shall hear, that shall he speak: and he will shew you things to come." John 16:13.

Human beings shouldn't judge God by their thoughts and by their own ways. God's activities transcend anything human beings could ever imagine. It is in the truth of God that we live move, and exist.

The Spirit of truth will continue the work of God. This means that all truth was given to the apostles by following Christ for three years of His ministry; they passed this truth to us through their writing and preaching and we still have the truth of the Scripture today.

The Holy Spirit discloses what is to come. He discloses the truth about you and concerning God's will and plan for your life. As believers understand more and more the Word of God and His ways, they will see and find out the meaning of their life and the direction in which God wants them to go for His glory. "For I know the thoughts that I think towards you, said the Lord, thoughts of peace, and not evil, to give you an expected end". Jer. 29:11.

The Holy Spirit glorifies Jesus Christ. As believers understand the Word of God and obey the Holy Spirit's voice, they glorify and bring honor to our Lord Jesus Christ and to God the Father. This is the believers' ultimate goal in life; their purpose in life is to live a life that will continuously glorify God's Holy Name.

The Apostle Paul said, "Whether therefore ye eat, or drink, or whatsoever ye do, do all to the glory of God." 1 Cor. 10:31. The main purpose of a believer's life is to please God and promote His glory. We have to do everything in honor of Him as our Lord, creator, and Redeemer King through our obedience, thankfulness, prayer, and loyalty. We have to live our life for the glory of our Lord and Savior.

"Likewise the Spirit also helpeth our infirmities: for we know not what we should pray for as we ought: but the Spirit itself maketh intercession for us with groanings which cannot be uttered." Rom. 8:26.

The Holy Spirit prays for us. Many believers face a time in their lives when they go through disappointment, difficulties, grief, or any number of uncertain circumstances when they don't feel like praying or don't know how to pray about their particular situation, which is very overwhelming, and they lack the words for prayer.

The Holy Spirit helps all believers in their prayers through important observations; as the children of God we have two divine intercessors. Christ intercedes for believers in heaven at the right hand of God where He is seated.

The Holy Spirit, who dwells in our hearts, intercedes for us on earth. Our spiritual desires and yearnings as believers are found in the Holy Spirit, who dwells within them. The Spirit pleads our case to the Father on behalf of our needs, in accordance with the will of God.

Our heavenly Father knows all of our needs and He has given us His Spirit to help us in all areas of our lives. The Holy Spirit bears witness with our spirit that we are the children of God. Sometimes, believers find themselves doubting, feeling that God is far away from them, or feeling that God does not care for them.

The spirit bears witness by reminding them of what God has said in His word. He brings some Bible verses into their remembrance. "We love Him, because He first loved us." 1 John 4:19. "Have I not commanded thee? Be strong and of a good courageous; be not afraid, neither be thou dismayed: for the Lord thy God is with thee whithersoever thou go." Jos. 1:9.

The Lord God Almighty was instructing His newly appointed servant that those who know and obey Him and His word and who follow the Law will have great success and that they will be prosperous and possess the wisdom to live righteously according to God's will for their lives.

The tool for great, successful living is achieved when the believer is very strong in the Lord and courageous and when the Word of God is the compass for their lives. "Casting all your care upon Him; for He careth for you." 1 Pet. 5:7.

Our God cares about the suffering and pain that every one of His children is going through; this truth is also emphasized through the Word of God. God knows all of our troubles, our sickness and pain, and our fears of enemies, especially those who are enemies of God.

Believers must hand it all over to Our Lord and Savior Jesus Christ. The Holy Spirit is there to testify or confirm that believers belong to God; they are the children of God and heirs to all that which belongs to Jesus Christ and God the Father Almighty. "The Spirit itself beareth witness with our spirit, that we are the sons of God. And if children, then heirs; and joint heirs with Christ; if so be that we suffer with him, that we may be also glorified together." Rom. 8:16-17.

The Holy Spirit is given as a pledge, as a promise. God promised all believers eternal life if they confess their sins and ask for the Savior Jesus Christ to come into their hearts. Their sins have been forgiven and they have been offered the promise to be with God for all eternity.

God offered this salvation to both Jews and Gentiles. Then, remember what the Lord said: "Wait for the promise of the Father, which ye have heard of me. For John truly baptized with water; but ye shall be baptized with the Holy Ghost not many days hence."

Forasmuch then, God gave them the same gift as he did to us, who believed in the Lord Jesus Christ, "What was I, that I could withstand God?" Acts 11:16-17. Peter told the leader of the early Church that God gave the same gift to the Gentiles as he gave to the apostles.

The disciples believed in Jesus Christ and they were regenerated by the Holy Spirit. The Gentiles were also included in Christ when they heard the word of truth, the Gospel of salvation. Once they believed, they were marked in Him with a seal, the promised Holy Spirit, who is the deposit guaranteeing their inheritance until the redemption of those who are in God's possession and praise His glory.

# 2

# Breath of the Son of God

"Receive Ye the Spirit." John 20:22. Christ elevated the apostles when He breathed on them, and said, receive ye the Holy Ghost. This sign not only show them, by this breath of life, that he himself was really alive, but to signify to them the spiritual life and power which they should receive from him.

As the breath of the Almighty God gave life to man and began the old world, same the breath of Christ signifies the power of his grace; the Spirit is the gift of Christ that Christ gave to the apostles, he conferred the Holy Spirit by the breathing for He is the author of the gift of the Holy Spirit.

He gave them the Holy Spirit then and the Spirit began working on them before the day of Pentecost. The breath of the Lord, at that time, was how He gave the apostles the power of the Holy Spirit, just as how

Moses had laid his hands on Joshua in the wilderness to continue leading the Israelites to the promised land. The breath transfers the power of the Holy Spirit to the apostles so that they may be able to obey and stay in Jerusalem before the day of Pentecost.

The breath also symbolizes how Elijah transferred power to Elisha before the Chariot of fire and horses of fire took him to heaven. "And it came to pass, when they were gone over, that Elijah said unto Elisha, ask what I shall do for thee, before I be taken away from thee. And Elisha said, I pray thee, let a double portion of thy spirit be upon me.

And he said, "Thou hast asked a hard thing: nevertheless, if thou see me when I am taken from thee, it shall be so unto thee; but if not, it shall not be so. And it came to pass, as they still went on, and talked, that, behold, there appeared a chariot of fire, and horses of fire, and parted them both asunder; and Elijah went up by a whirlwind into heaven. And he took the mantel of Elijah that fell from him, and smote the waters, and said, where is the Lord God of Elijah? And when he also had smitten the waters, they parted hither and thither: and Elisha went over." 2 Kings 2:9-10, 14.

We can easily see the power of the Holy Spirit in transporting Elijah to heaven by the whirlwind wind is one of the signs of the Holy Spirit. Just as the Spirit of God was hovering in the beginning of creation, all the apostles witnessed a rushing wind on the day of Pentecost when the power of the Holy Spirit descended upon them. The breath foreshadows the promise that would be fulfilled on the day of Pentecost. The breath empowers the great commission of Our Lord: "Go ye into all the nations." Luke 24:49.

The breath of our Lord causes the Spirit to be born in their hearts. The Holy Spirit hovered in the hearts of the apostles to bring them to life before the day of Pentecost; without the Spirit power we cannot obey the commandments of God.

Jesus connected the Holy Spirit to the forgiveness and repentance of sins, teaching the apostles of the preaching of repentance and forgiveness of sins. "And that repentance and the remission of sins should be preached in His name among all nations, beginning at Jerusalem." Luke 24:47.

When Jesus breathed on the apostles, they received the Holy Spirit but were not empowered until the day of Pentecost. As God breathed on Adam and Eve, "and the Lord God formed man of the dust of the ground, and breathed into his nostrils the breath of life; and man became a living soul." Gen. 2:7.

They became living beings; Jesus refers to the creation of the first man when he breathed His breath into the Apostles. He made them new creations, born of the Spirit of God. He repeated what He did in the Garden of Eden. God the Father spoke, God the Son created new life and God the Holy Spirit helped to sustain the new life by producing all the fruit of the Spirit that is needed for living a new life.

The breath of God the Father gave life to Adam and Eve and made them living beings; in the same way, Christ the Savior of the universe breathed on the apostles for the creation of a new world, which also indicated the Son's power on earth, as well as the gift of grace to all mankind.

The apostles became a new Spirit-filled, created being; Christ made them alive in Him. This was also applied to everyone who was present on that day, not only to the apostles. It has been shown from then on that in order to be a true Christian or believer of Jesus, one must receive the Holy Spirit regenerated, made alive, which we call born again.

Throughout the three years they spent following the Lord, they did not have the indwelling of the Spirit of God. The Spirit of God worked within them, producing the fruit of patience, strengthening them, increasing their faith, and making them true and strong in the Lord so that they could live a spiritual life.

The Spirit of God made the Gospel alive in their heart. The Spirit opened their understanding of the Gospel Scriptures and enabled them to teach others or explain them to other people around them.

Otherwise, on the day of Pentecost, they would not have been able to preach to people to the extent that three thousand people were converted on that day.

For example, Thomas was not with the Apostles when the Lord breathed on them. Thomas, one of the twelve, called Didymus, was not with them when Jesus came. But he said unto them, "Unless I shall see in his hands the print of nails, and put my finger into the print of the nails, and thrust my hand into his side, I will not believe." John 20:24-25b.

"After eight days the disciples were gather together and Thomas was with them: then came, Jesus, the doors being shut, and stood in the midst, and said, Peace be unto you." John 20:26.

While Jesus was talking to Thomas, He opened his understanding and the Spirit of God was upon him Jesus made him alive in Him. This continues to happen even until today; many people are struggling to live a Christian life. Because they did not have the indwelling of the Holy Spirit, they are always confused, with guilt and doubts.

Some of them will say they believe in God but not in Jesus, and they usually remain like that until someone prays for them and opens the Scripture to them. Then, the Holy Spirit will be able to manifest His power to them as He did to the sinners.

This makes it clear what the Bible says, "Jesus answered and said unto him, Verily, verily, I say unto thee, except a man be born again, and he cannot see the kingdom of God." John 3:3. The first blessing of our Lord after His resurrection and before His ascension was the blessing of new birth, or, the regeneration of the apostles. Christ breathes on them and they become new creations, Spirit-filled beings.

The Spirit of God brought back the apostles to spiritual life from their spiritual death; they received forgiveness of all their sins and began Holy lives. God's breath made the first creation. Likewise, Jesus' breath made the new creation and God's breath to Adam gave him life.

In the new creation, Christ breathed into the apostles and gave them eternal life, life everlasting, which is different from the case of Adam and Eve. A brand-new creation, "Therefore if any man be in Christ, he is a new creature: old things are passed away; behold, all things are become new." 2 Cor. 5:17.

He becomes a new creature in Christ, through the creative command of God. Those who accept Jesus Christ through faith are made into a new creation that belongs to God's total new earth in which the Spirit of God rules.

Christ also blessed them with the Spirit of peace. The Holy Spirit worked and produced the fruit of peace in the disciples before the day of Pentecost. "Peace be unto you." John 20:26.

Christ, through the Holy Spirit, always blesses the believer with the gift of the Holy Spirit and with the fruit of the Holy Spirit, which is peace. The Peace of God rules in the hearts and minds of those who have been persecuted, afflicted, and hurt, and of those who are in trouble due to many different circumstances.

He blesses believers with peace to be strong, to be strengthened, to not be afraid, to be strong and immovable, to have unshakable faith, to be courageous, and to stand firm in the Lord. He blesses the apostles with peace so that they may wait for His promise. The third blessing of our Lord occurred when He breathed on them and He said, "receive the Holy Spirit's joy."

"And ye now therefore have sorrow: but I will see you again, and your heart shall rejoice, and your joy no man taketh from you." John 16:22.

Our Lord wants the apostles to rejoice in what has happened and what is still going to happen the result is that they rejoice in the joy He is giving them, which is a joy that cannot be taken away from them. All believers share the same joy today, which is the joy of resurrection and eternal life.

The apostles were overjoyed to see the Lord after he was crucified, dead, and buried; they never knew that they could see Him again. He was alive, eating, and speaking with them. Jesus compared the pain of the apostles to a woman who was in pain of childbirth and rejoiced, full of joy, after the child was born.

"A woman when she is in travail hath sorrow, because her hour is come: but as soon as she is delivered of the child, she remembereth no more the anguish, for joy that a man is born into the world." John 16:21.

Breathing on the apostles brought great joy to them and showed that the Spirit would produce the fruit of joy and peace on the apostles. The fourth blessing of Jesus' breath on the apostles was the blessing of the power of the Holy Spirit to bear witness.

The Spirit produced in them, before the day of Pentecost, power to proclaim the gospel to unbelievers for forgiveness of their sins. "Then said Jesus to them again, Peace be unto you: as my Father hath sent me, even so send I you." John 20:21.

The Father sends Jesus, His only begotten Son, to save the world. Jesus Christ sent the apostles and all of the body of Christ on earth to continue this great commission. The peace that the Spirit of God produces takes away fear, confusion, and sadness, and calms down believers' fear and confusion. The Spirit gave and produced courage and brought peace of God to the believers' spirit, soul, and body.

The Holy Spirit shed His light and produced strength, ability, and power for the apostles, before the day of Pentecost, to witness and boldly proclaim the gospel of God to all people on the day of Pentecost.

On that day, the apostles were filled with great power, to such an extent that three thousand sinners were converted. Everyone that has the Spirit of God in him or her has a burden for missionary work, for saving sinners and calling the lost unto Christ. This is the automatic work of the Holy Spirit, to make believers strive for the work of the Gospel and to take the Gospel of God to the ends of the earth.

Believers become God's workmanship through the Holy Spirit; they are new creations in Christ Jesus. They are very unique and placed into the body of Christ, regardless of whether they are Jews or Gentiles, black or white.

Regardless of their ethnicity or nationality, believers share one Spirit of Jesus Christ and they are one body of Christ. Believers are created in Christ Jesus to do the good work that Spirit of God has assigned to them before the beginning of creation.

Believers belong to a glorious new creation, which God, through the power of the Holy Spirit, has brought into his existing plan of redemption and salvation through Jesus Christ His Son.

# 3

# Holy Spirit Power in the New Testament

One important aspect of the Holy Spirit in the New Testament is that God is available to every believer through baptism with the Holy Spirit. Every believer must be filled with the power of the Holy Spirit.

The Spirit has given us the power to witness the Gospel to people who have never heard the Gospel before. We do our witnessing as commanded and the Holy Spirit carries out the transformation.

The Spirit of God will transform the non-believing sinner into a child of God. The Holy Spirit empowers believers against the enemy: "Ye are of God, little children, and have overcome them: because greater is he that is in you, than he that is in the world." 1 John 4:4. This verse is telling us that: the Spirit of God dwells in us and that Spirit is more mighty than men or devils. The Spirit of God has framed our mind for God and heaven.

The world will love its own, and its own will love it. The Holy Spirit indwelling is more powerful than Satan and the Devil. The Holy Spirit will convict us of sin, "Nevertheless I tell you the truth; it is expedient for you that I go away: for if I go not away, the Comforter will not come unto you; but if I depart, I will send him unto you. And when he is come, he will reprove the world of sin, and of righteousness, and of judgment." John 16:7-8.

The outpouring of the Holy Spirit occurred after Christ went to heaven. The Holy Spirit's principal work with respect to proclaiming the Gospel will be that of convicting sin. The Holy Spirit will expose sin and unbelief in order to awaken a consciousness of guilt and need for forgiveness.

The Spirit will let us know when we are doing bad things or about to do bad things either to ourselves or to other people around us. The Holy Spirit is our director and controller. He convicts us of sin or warns us of sin before we commit it.

In this, the Spirit helps us to maintain a close relationship with our Lord. After the conviction of sin, true repentance always happens and turning to Christ as Lord and Savior prevails. In order to access the Spirit power, we must be baptized with the Holy Spirit. Each believer needs to be filled with the Holy Spirit every day by following the words of God. The role of the ministry of the Holy Spirit in our lives is to keep us away from the work of the flesh.

The most important thing is that the Holy Spirit has the power to control our lives. One of the powers of the Holy Spirit with regard to believers is the ability to bear witness and to provide strength for performing an activity related to the work of the Gospel.

An example is the day of Pentecost: "And there appeared unto them cloven tongues like as of fire, and it sat upon each of them and they were all filled with the Holy Ghost, and began to speak with other tongues, as the Spirit gave them utterance." Acts 2:3-4.

First, on the day of Pentecost, there was a sound like the flowing of a violent wind as a sign that the Holy Spirit came with power. Second, there was a sign that appeared visibly: the tongues of fire that rested on each of the disciples, indicating the prophetic symbol that the Holy Spirit was coming to empower them.

Third, they began to speak in foreign languages to the people that came from different countries in their own native languages. The disciples knew clearly that Jesus Christ fulfilled His word of promise from His ascended position as exalted Lord and Christ at the Father's right hand of authority.

It assured them of the beginning of the Church. The disciples were clothed with the power of God from above which enabled them to boldly bear witness for Christ to the people of different nations in their own languages. The disciples became ministers of the Spirit. They not only preached about Jesus' crucifixion and resurrection, leading to humankind's repentance and faith in Christ, but they also influenced converts to receive the gift of the Holy Spirit.

Leading people to baptism in the Holy Spirit is the key to the apostolic work described in the New Testament. Through this baptism in the Spirit, Christ's followers became the successors to his earthly ministry.

All Christians continued to act and teach, through the power of the Holy Spirit, the same things that Jesus had begun to do and to teach. The Holy Spirit is God's agent for purifying and illuminating believers.

The main work of the Holy Spirit is to continuously pour power upon the believer. Baptism is an act of obedience in the life of every believer in Jesus Christ, which also leads to the power to commit and proclaim the Gospel of God.

It is also a means of public identification of believers to Jesus Christ following His death, burial, and resurrection "Know ye not, that so many of us as were baptized into Jesus Christ were baptized into his death?

Therefore we are buried with him by baptism into death: that like as Christ was raised up from the dead by the glory of the Father, even so we also should walk in newness of life." Rom. 6:3-4. "Then Peter said unto them, Repent, and be baptized every one of you in the name of Jesus Christ for the remission of sins, and ye shall receive the gift of the Holy Ghost." Acts 2:38.

"Not by works of righteousness which we have done, but according to his mercy he saved us, by the washing of regeneration, and renewing of the Holy Ghost." Titus 3:5.

The spiritual renewal of Christ's believers refers to the new birth of believers, symbolically pictured in all Christians' baptisms. Renewal by the Holy Spirit points to the constant imparting of His life to believers as they surrender their lives to God through Jesus Christ.

The Holy Spirit's appearance in the Gospel of John is the power by which Christians are brought by faith and it is the Spirit that helps believers to understand their walk with God.

The Holy Spirit leads people to a new birth in Christ. "That which is born of the flesh is flesh; and that which is born of the Spirit is spirit." John 3:6. It is the Spirit who gave life to the converted sinners and made them Christians.

"It is the Spirit that quickeneth; the flesh profiteth nothing: the words that I speak unto you, they are Spirit, and they are life." John 6:63. The early Church confirmed the Holy Spirit's work as baptisms occurred within the outpouring of the Spirit's power in the missionary and evangelical work.

The Holy Spirit reveals to believers the profound nature of God and the mystery of Christ. Being baptized by the Holy Spirit means being led by the Spirit, following the Word of God, and thinking with the mind of God. Our Lord made a promise to the disciples of the Holy Spirit, and his promise was fulfilled ten days after His ascension into heaven on the day of Pentecost.

Then, the Holy Spirit was sent from God the Father by Jesus Christ, and all of the apostles were filled with the Holy Spirit. This was also the day when the Church of Christ was born on earth. The apostles were filled with supernatural power, to the extent that they were speaking in foreign languages.

Many people heard them speaking in their own languages and were amazed. The same Spirit of God that indwelled Jesus throughout His earthly ministry, also indwelled all of the apostles, who were able to powerfully continue the Gospel ministry through the power of the Spirit, just as our Lord had done when He was with them.

The disciples already believed. They knew that Christ was the Son of God, the Messiah who was to come; but they needed power from above in order to carry out the work of the ministry.

Even today, all of Christ's believers need the working power of the Spirit of God for the miracle of converting sinners and the lost. Jesus Christ wants all believers to abide in Him so that they can live and walk within the supernatural power of the Holy Spirit. Believers must be born of the Spirit of God, before they can be baptized with the Spirit. Many believers have been saved but were not baptized with the Holy Spirit.

For example, this was the case of the believers in Samaria during the apostles' era. They were saved but not baptized with the Holy Spirit until Apostle Peter laid hands on them. "Now when the apostles which were at Jerusalem heard that Samaria had received the Word of God, they sent unto them Peter and John: When they came down, they prayed for them, that they might receive the Holy Ghost." Acts 8:14-15.

"He that believeth and is baptized shall be saved; but he that believeth not shall be damned." Mark 16:16. "And Ananias went his way, and entered into the house; and putting his hands on him said, Brother Saul, the Lord even Jesus, that appeared unto thee on the way as thou camest, hath sent me, that thou mightiest receive thy sight, and be filled with the Holy Ghost." Acts 9:17.

These two examples make it very clear that the conversion of believers is different from baptism, or the infilling of the Holy Spirit. There are times that people will be converted and at the same time receive the baptism of the Holy Spirit the Spirit of God work differently in the lives of individual believers of Christ.

An example of when people received the baptism of the Holy Spirit was revealed in Cornelius, "While Peter yet spake these words, the Holy Ghost fell on all them which heard the word." Acts 10:44. Cornelius and his entire household were Gentiles. As they listened and received the word with saving faith and acceptance of Christ, God at once poured out the Holy Spirit on them, bearing witness that they believed and had received the regenerating life of Christ.

The outpouring of the Holy Spirit on Cornelius and his household has the same purpose as the gift of the Spirit had for the disciples on the day of Pentecost. The outpouring of the Holy Spirit came upon them also with power from above, just as it did on the day of Pentecost.

As Peter was preaching, the Spirit power fell on the entire household. The regenerative work of the Holy Spirit and the baptismal work of the Holy Spirit are two different distinct works of the Spirit of God.

Each of these works of the Spirit results in the manifestation of the presence of God in the life of the believer. We must know very well that those manifestations are not the same and that our Lord made this clear in the Gospel of John, who was one of the apostles who witnessed and experienced this distinction of the Spirit Power.

"But whosoever drinketh of the water that I shall give him shall never thirst; but the water that I shall give him shall, be in him a well of water springing up into everlasting life." John 4:14.

Jesus was at the well speaking to the Samaritan woman. He was referring to the indwelling of the Holy Spirit in the lives of believer when they were born again and converted, because water is one of the signs of the power of the Holy Spirit.

Drinking the water of life requires regular communion with the source of the living water: Jesus Christ Himself. No one can continue to drink the water of life if he or she becomes severed from its source. The act of drinking is not a momentary act or single occurrence, but rather a progressive or repeated, continuous act of drinking.

The Spirit indwelling is like water bubbling up for eternal life. When believers have the indwelling of the Spirit, it is like a well of water, full of the spiritual power of God that sustains and holds believers to God in the face of any earthly obstacles.

Regarding the river of the living waters, God said, "He that believeth on me, as the scripture hath said, out of his belly shall flow rivers of living water." John 7:38.

Christ was referring to the Scripture because it was the very Word of God and, therefore, the supreme authority for His life and teaching. The Scripture is also the supreme authority for Christians, for God alone has the right to determine our standards of conduct.

He has chosen to exercise this authority by making his truth known in Scripture. The Bible is God's revelation; it carries the same authority as if God Himself were speaking to us directly. The inspired scriptures are the believer's ultimate authority.

The Ecclesiastical traditions, prophecies, doctrines, and human ideas must be tested against the Scripture and should never be elevated to a place of equal authority with the Bible. Therefore, all those who are unwilling to submit their beliefs to the lordship of Jesus Christ by submitting them to the authority of the New Testament, place themselves outside of Biblical revelation and salvation in Christ alone.

When the gift of the Spirit power is given to believers, they will experience His overflowing life. The living water will also miraculously overflow within them to other people around them with the healing message of Jesus Christ.

The difference between the well and the river is that the well is the Spirit power inside the believer that provides him or her with strength in order to be obedient to the Lord and control and to help him or her to live a Christian life.

The river of the living water is the power of the Holy Spirit that strengthens the believer so that God's Spirit may flow like a river inside of him, which also flows within him so that he may carry out many ministry works.

In the Old Testament, baptism in the spirit occurred when the Israelites crossed the Jordan River into the Promised Land and passed through the Red Sea, symbolizing baptism and deliverance from the other nations.

"And the children of Israel went into the midst of the sea upon the dry ground: and the waters were a wall unto them on their right hand, and on their left." Exo. 14:22.

"And as they that bare the ark were come unto Jordan, and the feet of the priests that bare the ark were dipped in the brim of the water, for Jordan over floweth all his banks all the time of harvest, that the waters which came down from above stood and rose up upon an heap very far from that city Adam.

"That is beside Zaretan: and those that came down toward the sea of the plain, even the salt came sea, failed, and were cut off: and the people passed over right against Jericho." Jos. 3:15-16.

God divided the flood water in Jordan, just as he had divided the Red Sea. This miracle was visible evidence that God was with Joshua, just as he had been with Moses. The Jordan River was parted so that the Israelites could go through; God exercised His miraculous power again by parting the Jordan River for the Israelites to pass through.

This also symbolizes baptism in the Holy Spirit in the lives of the people of God in the present day. All Jesus Christ's believers were indwelled with the power of the Holy Spirit. God's Spirit is upon all children of God and those who believe in Him. The Spirit of God helps, controls, directs, and guides them. By this experiential demonstration of the Spirit of God's power, people's faith is strengthened. They were able to face the challenges of possessing the Promised Land.

Without such miraculous power of the Holy Spirit of God, they could not have taken the walled cities and advanced forward, in spite of the numerous oppositions that they faced when they arrived at their new land.

Today, God's Spirit continues to fight His believers' battles in all areas of our lives, when we are not even aware of his actions; the Spirit of God also testifies, "For ye have not received the spirit of bondage again fear; but ye have received the Spirit of adoption, whereby we cry, Abba, Father.

The Spirit itself beareth witness with our spirit, that we are the children of God." Rom. 8:15-16. The Holy Spirit imparts to us the confidence that through Christ and with Christ, we are now God's children. He makes real the truth that Christ loves us and that He lives for us in heaven as our mediator.

The Spirit also shows us that the Father loves us as His adopted children, no less than He loves His one and only Son. The Spirit creates in us the love and confidence by which we cry to Him as our Father with all of our problems.

The born again Christians are like water in the well, while those who are baptized in the Spirit receive the Spirit empowerment which is the Spirit water as a river. Baptism in the Spirit operates in believers' lives as a great manifestation of the presence of God, which empowers believers with the fullness of the power of God.

"But ye shall receive power, after that the Holy Ghost is come upon you: and ye shall be witnesses unto me both in Jerusalem, and in all Judea, and in Samaria, and unto the uttermost part of the earth." Acts 1:8.

Our Lord told the apostles on the day of His ascension, before He ascended into heaven, that they would receive power from above. The primary purpose of baptism in the spirit is to receive power in order to bear witness for Christ so that the lost will be won over to Him and taught to obey all that Christ has commanded.

It is most important for Jesus Christ to be known, love, praised, and made the Lord of God's chosen people. Power means more than strength or ability; it especially implies power in operation, in action, to do the Gospel's work. It also includes the authority to drive out evil spirits. Witnessing and anointing to heal the sick are the two essential signs accompanying the proclamation of God's kingdom.

It means the power to testify, to perform miracles in so many ways that unbelievers will know that Christ is the true Son of God. Baptism in the Holy Spirit is for the work of the ministry, the work of the gospel, witnessing, preaching, teaching, healing, and praying. It is given to those who believe and this power of the Holy Spirit is still available today to all believers who meet all of the requirements for receiving it. It was poured out on the day of Pentecost and it is still available to all believers today.

It is available to those who ask for it after they have been born again, abide in Christ, follow His commandments, and are obedient to the Spirit's control. Our Lord said, "If ye then, being evil, know how to give good gifts unto your children: how much more shall your heavenly Father give the Holy Spirit to them that ask him?" Luke 11:13.

Our Lord was not referring to the impartation of the Spirit, whose indwelling presence was given automatically to believers upon their conversion; rather, He was referring to the baptism in the Holy Spirit that He promised to all believers to whom he promised power from above.

The baptism in the Holy Spirit is a gift from God the Father through God the Son. "And, being assembled together with them, commanded them that they should not depart from Jerusalem, but wait for the promise of the Father, which, said he, ye have heard of me." Acts 1:4.

Christ reminded the disciples of the gift from the Father, which is the baptism in the Holy Spirit. The fulfillment of the promise was described as being filled with the Holy Spirit; therefore, being baptized in the Spirit and filled with the Spirit are, at times, used interchangeably.

This baptism in the Holy Spirit should not be identified with receiving the Holy Spirit upon regeneration. These are two distinct works of the Spirit, often separated by a period of time after the conversion of Jesus Christ's believers.

It is the grace of God not that we deserve it or are worthy of it. It is a blessing from the Lord for the work of the gospel. It has nothing to do with age, or with being a pastor, minister, or priest. It is the outpouring gift of God to believers, after they have been born again and are fully part of the body of Christ.

There is no other way to earn baptism in the Holy Spirit; God gives it when believers ask for it. Our Lord Jesus Christ sent the Holy Spirit to empower the entire body of Christ, in order for them to be able to carry out the work of the kingdom with the power of the Spirit and to proclaim the gospel of God boldly, clearly, confidently, and with great power.

The Church must not wait; they must carry out the work that Christ as assigned to them with the power of the Holy Spirit. The early Church concentrated on the power of the Spirit of God to complete this work we believers today must do the same.

We must do everything in accordance with the Spirit Power that God is sends to us for His glory and take the Gospel of God to the ends of the earth for Christ. The work of the ministry must be done with the Spirit Power of miracles, signs, and wonders. Our Lord said, "greater work than this shall you do. Stay in Jerusalem until you receive the power from on high." Baptism in the Holy Spirit is for all of Jesus Christ's believers. All Christians have the Spirit indwelling power active in their lives, as a well of water bubbling up for eternal life.

God the Father's will is for all believers to have the Spirit power flowing within them as river of water, the river of the living water, so that the Spirit of God will be able to exercise His power, exhibit His power, extend His grace in every detail, exhibit His infinite love, and manifest His power to flow through believers like a river to sinners, the lost, unbelievers, and all other people of different religions.

When the power of the Holy Spirit begins to flow with supernatural power, things will begin to happen in the world. The conversion of souls will begin to happen; every minute, everywhere, Christians will witness, the souls of unbelievers will be converted, the Gospel of God will be preached, and believers will be able to work as tent-makers or boldly witness to the lost and to sinners.

Believers will be able to serve the Lord with joy because they have the supernatural power of the Holy Spirit flowing within them, energizing them. All of Jesus Christ's believers must be baptized in the Holy Spirit in order to serve the Lord from this earth to heaven. "What are we waiting for?" He said, "Ask and you shall be given." Though all Christians are indwelled with the Holy Spirit, not all Christians are filled, directed, and empowered by the Holy Spirit.

The Holy Spirit is the source of overflowing life. "In the last day, that great day of the feast, Jesus stood and cried, saying, if any man thirst, let him come unto me, and drink. He that believeth on me, as the scripture hath said, out of his belly shall flow rivers of living water." John 7:37-38.

This means that when the gift of the Spirit is given to believers, they will experience Christ's overflowing life. The living water will flow out from deep, within the believer to others, with the healing message of Jesus Christ. If any man desires Spiritual blessings, Spiritual happiness, let him come to Christ. He will fill the thirsty souls that come to Him with the water of life.

# 4

# The Spirit Power
# at Pentecost

On the day of Pentecost, the power and the filling of the Holy Spirit became available to all who accepted Christ, which means all who had been born in the Spirit.

"Jesus answered and said unto him, Verily, verily I say unto thee, Except a man be born again, he cannot see the kingdom of God. Nicodemus said unto him, how can a man be born when he is old?

"Can he enter the second time into his mother's womb, and be born? Jesus answered, Verily, verily, I say unto thee, except a man be born of water and of the Spirit, he cannot enter into the kingdom of God. That which is born of the flesh is flesh, and that which is born of the Spirit is Spirit.

"Marvel not that I said unto thee, Ye must be born again. The wind bloweth where it listed, and thou hearest the sound thereof, but canst not tell whence it cometh, and whither it goeth: so is every one that is born of the Spirit." John 3:3-8.

Only believers can experience this power. Being filled by the Spirit is conditional, a believer may decide to be filled or not to be filled it depends and is based only on the believer's relationship with our Lord and Savior Christ.

Not all believers are filled with the Spirit. Our closeness to the Lord is measured by our filling with the Spirit, in order to see which one of the Holy Spirit's fruits we use every day, which one do we need to use more, and which one will change us completely to what God wants us to be in this world.

If there is any area in the believer's life where the fruit of the Spirit is not exercised, the believer must do all he or she can to make sure that the particular fruit is utilized: either by reading the Word of God or by consciously putting it into action.

Most believers want to know how can they be more filled with the Holy Spirit, but God has given them the fullness of his Spirit all they need to do is to use it and the only way that they will be able to use it is to stay in the Word of God, pray more and more, and put everything into his Holy hands.

When believers maintain an intimate, close, and pure relationship with the Lord they will automatically be empowered by the Holy Spirit. Everything they do through the power of the Holy Spirit will be manifest and they will see the glory of our Lord and Savior shining upon them in a way that has never occurred before in their lives as believers of Jesus Christ.

Believers must strengthen their relationship with the Lord in order to be empowered by the Spirit of God. Believers must ask for the presence of the Holy Spirit whenever they kneel down to pray; they must also ask for the Spirit of discernment in order to know the difference between the spirit of error and the spirit of truth.

They must ask for the full presence of the Holy Spirit. Once the Spirit fill us up, or, once we are filled by the Spirit and anointed, all we need to do is to ask and it shall be given, in accordance with our heavenly Father's Will.

Most of the time, the Holy Spirit speaks to us through the Word of God, through our heart, and through so many other means that we can only know or be aware of them through the Spirit of discernment.

By remaining within the Word of God and studying the Word of God, through worship, singing praises, and dancing, we will receive the Spirit's enablement, which will empower us and help us to resist temptation and any other obstacles that might try to overcome us.

Believers need to be conscious of the Holy Spirit at all times in order to grow in the Lord. "And we, who with unveiled faces all reflect the Lord's glory, are being transformed into his likeness with ever increasing glory, which comes from the Lord, who is the Spirit." 2 Cor. 3:18.

All believers, all Christians, as we experience Christ's closeness, love, righteousness, and power through prayer and the Holy Spirit, we are transformed into his likeness. "For God, who commanded, the light shine out of darkness, hath shined in our hearts, to give the light of the knowledge of the glory of God in the face of Jesus Christ." 2 Cor. 4:6.

The Scripture tells us that we are changed into the likeness or image of what we behold, look at, and think about. Right now, at the present time, the transformation is progressive and not yet complete. When Christ returns, we will see him face-to-face and our transformation will be complete.

Believers are the body of Christ, which means that we are His Church on this earth. The Holy Spirit equips and enables us to bear witness to the people of the world, through the gifts of the Spirit; when we are filled with the Spirit we produce the fruit of the Spirit.

The Spirit manifests itself in our life to benefit individual believers as one Church, one body, one baptism, and one Lord. In this way, every believer will receive the gift of the Holy Spirit and the entire body of Christ will be complete in him and be able to benefit from the blessing that comes every day to the entire body of Christ—His Church on earth.

When we come to Christ, we receive power because God's Holy Spirit indwells us. God empowers us to take the Gospel of Jesus Christ to the ends of the earth. The entire body of Christ is commissioned we must fulfill Christ's great commission.

The closer we get to the image of Christ through the transforming power of the Holy Spirit, the more we will be able to carry out this great commission. "And he that searcheth the hearts knoweth what is the mind of the Spirit, because he maketh intercession for us with groanings which cannot be uttered." Rom. 8:27.

The Spirit of Jesus Christ searches our hearts and intercedes according to the will of God; the will of God is to bear witness to sinners, the lost, and unbelievers. Not all believers allow the Holy Spirit to indwell them or affect their lives in order to live within God's moral directives through the indwelling of the Holy Spirit.

For example, one of God's moral directives says, "do not commit adultery." Because of their immoral lifestyle, they do not want to be indwelled by the Holy Spirit. Some believers continue to live in sin, struggling to overcome temptation on their own.

Their lives are not, and will not, be fulfilled without the Holy Spirit; they will not experience the joy of the living heart that the Holy Spirit produced and provided to believers.

The main reason believers must be filled with the spirit is to be able to engage in all spiritual activities, all of the Holy Spirit's activities in the world. The second reason for believers be filled with the Holy Spirit is to be able to live in heaven from earth by setting their minds on heavenly things.

When believers are filled with the Holy Spirit, they will have a sense of the love, joy, and peace that the Holy Spirit produces in the lives of the believer. A spirit-filled Christian who possesses all the fruits of the Spirit will be different from other Christians who are not possessed with the fruits of the Holy Spirit.

When Christians are filled with the Spirit, or when the Holy Spirit lives inside or indwells Christians, the Spirit will guide the actions and desires of the believer, or Christians.

The Spirit empowers believers to step outside of their comfort zone to do supernatural and extraordinary things through their faith in God, which will make everyone, or the world, be completely surprised or amazed.

Believers will have the mind of Christ and a sense of partnership with Christ in His work of redemption and in the work of the kingdom, as well as in many of God's plans concerning His creations and His created beings.

The inner power of the Holy Spirit has power over the hearts of men and women. No minister or pastor can win the hearts of men and women by himself. A pastor can win the ears of people and make them listen;

he can win their eyes and cause them to look at him; and, he can win their attention.

Yet, their hearts are very slippery, like a fish that all Gospel fishermen find difficult to hold on to—sometimes almost pulling it out of the water, but it slips between their fingers, and evades capture. Many ministers and pastors have been disappointed in this endeavor.

They wonder why that particular person did not come forward and give their life to Christ after preaching. They have been terribly disappointed. They do not know whether to study more or go through the scripture more. They've wondered where they went wrong, what they should have said and did not say, and approach they have missed in their preaching.

Then they will come to the realization and remember that the Word of God says, "Not by might nor by power, but by my Spirit says the Lord Almighty." Zec. 4:6. The Holy Spirit is the only one who has the power to change the heart or power over the hearts of men and women, young or old.

A minister cannot convert the soul. A minister cannot touch the heart or break through to the hearts of men, for it is difficult. A minister cannot reach the soul of a human being. Yet, the Holy Spirit can change the heart of human being in a minute, turning the heart of stone into a heart of flesh. The Holy Spirit will wash a sinner with the precious blood of Jesus and the person will become new. The Holy Spirit can touch the hearts of men and women and make them perform the impossible in their lives.

He can turn the heart of an Atheist non-believer who says there is no God to a preacher of the Word of God. The Holy Spirit can turn the heart of the pagan idol-worshiper to begin teaching and proclaiming the Gospel of God all over the earth.

There is no limit to what the Spirit of God can do in the lives of men and women on this earth. The Holy Spirit has power over the heart, soul, and body. Another inner spiritual power of the Holy Spirit is the will of men and women, which has been called the freewill.

Freewill made Adam and Eve fall in the Garden of Eden. Freewill also made a third of the angels in heaven fall into Hell or the abyss. Freewill can be used to do evil or to do good, to sin or not to sin.

"One man can bring a horse to the water, but hundred men cannot make him to drink." Proverb of John Haywood 1546. No man has power over his brother or fellow creature's will, but the Spirit of God does.

The Holy Spirit will make an unwilling sinner willing to take the Gospel or to learn more and more about the Gospel and make him run to the cross at the feet of Jesus Christ.

The Holy Spirit will make people who have laughed at Jesus and Christians to ask Christ for mercy. The unbeliever will be willing to believe through the power of the Holy Spirit. The unbeliever will gladly rejoice at the sound of the name of Jesus, through the powers of the Holy Spirit.

He is very delighted to obey God's commandments to do God's Word in every area of his life. The Holy Spirit of God is the only one that has the power to change the will of men and women, in order to turn them from hatred to love, from evil to good.

Another inner spiritual war is thought, which we have called imagination, which is difficult to control. The imagination sometimes goes through a power struggle with God. It is very hard to manage.

It can raise people up and it can bring them down. The Holy Spirit is the one who has power over our thought and everything we could imagine. The Holy Spirit's power clears all unnecessary thoughts, all of our imagination that come to us unawares, which we cannot control sometimes.

We always cry out to God to help us. The Holy Spirit of God is the only one who can conquer our imagination, and He will continue to do so throughout eternity. The Holy Spirit works on the imagination here on earth to control and suppress all of the thoughts that plague every human being.

The future work of the Holy Spirit is to perfect us to holiness. There are two kinds of perfection in the lives of Christians. Christians need perfection of justification through faith in the person of Jesus Christ, and, additionally, perfection of sanctification, which is the work of the Holy Spirit in the lives of believers.

Many people are still full of sin and their lives are of a sinful nature. Many Christians are not complete in Christ—their heart is particularly impure, they lust in all kinds of sexual immoralities, and they have greed and evil thoughts.

We have to rejoice because Christ is our hope of the glory of the day, that will come after not very long, when God will complete what He started in the lives of men and women. He will present believers as a perfect bride to the bridegroom Jesus, perfect in the Spirit with no blemishes or spots, presented at the feet of God without impurities or contamination.

Believers will be able to say on that great day that the glorious day is our God. We have been cleansed through the blood of Jesus; through the work of the Holy Spirit we are clean. Believers must praise the power of the Holy Spirit for making us fit to stand before the throne of grace, before our Father in heaven through the love and mercy of God.

The power of the Holy Spirit will continue to pour out to unbelievers and sinners. The Holy Spirit will continue to be poured out in a wonderful way; it will go everywhere to increase knowledge and understanding of the Lord on earth, just as water fills the sea.

Another future work of the Holy Spirit that will become manifest is the resurrection of all Christians.

The resurrection of the dead, using the same power that raised Jesus Christ from the dead, will cause mortal bodies to come to life. The power of the resurrection is the greatest work of the Holy Spirit. The Bible says, "Yes, in a moment at the twinkling of an eye, at the last trumpet the dead will be raised." 2 Thes. 4:16-17.

They are alive—see them scattered. Bones comes to their bones see their bare skeletons. Flesh comes onto them see them still and lifeless, coming from the four corners of the earth when the wind of the Holy Spirit comes. They live, and they stand up on their feet, a very great army of saints.

The Holy Spirit is very powerful. Believers must ask for the power of the Holy Spirit for protection he is omnipotent and all powerful. God's kingdom will come on earth, as it is written in heaven. His will, will be done on earth as it is set up in heaven.

People will see miraculous holiness, extraordinary power of prayer, real communion with God, free religion, and the spreading of the doctrines of the cross. Everyone will see that, truly, the Holy Spirit is poured out like water, just as rain descends from heaven.

The Holy Spirit of God will do all these things and more with his power. Believers need the power of the Holy Spirit to overcome our enemies, and to conquer the power of darkness and evil in our life. The power of the Holy Spirit is our power; the power of the Holy Spirit is our strength. Believers must not doubt the power of the Holy Spirit in their lives. The answers to our prayers might be delayed, yet we must wait for Him.

There is power in the Holy Spirit that conquers violence and all spiritual wickedness. The power of the Holy Spirit will make you strong enough to do the impossible; it will take care of all of the flocks, the lost, and the needy.

The Holy Spirit will continue to be poured out from above until the thirsty water is covered with springs of water and the desert blossom becomes like roses. The power of the Holy Spirit is able to do so many things that we cannot even imagine.

See the power of the Holy Spirit in the missions' field. See it in the tracts given on the side of the street, bringing sinners to Christ in a simple way, by reading the two lines of the tracts. The power of the Holy Spirit bears witness to Christian outreaching.

The power of the Holy Spirit is a great help to us in all the areas of our lives. Through the power of the Holy Spirit, there is hope for the chief of sinners; the power of the Holy Spirit can save you and your entire household.

The power of the Holy Spirit is able to break your rock hard heart—your eyes will run with tears even though they were rocks before. The power of the Holy Spirit changes the hearts of sinners and immediately makes you born again, blesses you with new spirit, new heart, and a new name and, moreover, makes you a child of God.

"Behold, what manner of love the father has bestowed upon us that we should be called the sons of God there the world knows us not, because it knew him not." 1 John 3:1.

To save a sinner in Christ, there is more than enough power. There is unlimited power in the Holy Spirit. Bring those who are weak and strong to Christ— the power of the Holy Spirit will overpower your free-will to make you yearn and be thirsty for Jesus and His righteousness.

All believers in Christ must put their trust in the power of the Holy Spirit and rest and rejoice in the blood of Jesus who can make their souls safe, now and for eternity. The Holy Spirit united us with Christ at the moment of our conversion.

Through his power, he causes us to believe in the gospel. All of us are able to experience the life-changing power of the Holy Spirit because the changing power of the Holy Spirit has the ability to be present every-where, in every place, at the same time.

"Where can I go from your spirit? Where can I flee from your presence." Psl. 139:7. When Jesus ascended to heaven, He promised that He would always be with us. And so He is, through the power of the Holy Spirit. Jesus and the Father dwell in us, as does the Holy Spirit.

The Holy Spirit will change our lives if we so permit Him. But remember, apart from Jesus we will never experience the fullness of life that God promises.

If you have the Spirit without the Word, you will blow up; if you have the Word without the Spirit, you will dry up; but, if you have both the Word and the Spirit, you will grow up. You will be refreshed and continue to grow.

# 5

# Inner Spiritual Power of the Holy Spirit

Another inner spiritual power of the Holy Spirit is the will of men and women, which has been called the Freewill. Freewill made Adam and Eve fall in the Garden of Eden.

Freewill also made a third of the angels in heaven fall into Hell or the Abyss. Freewill can be used to do evil or to do good, to sin or not to sin. No man has power over his brother or fellow creature's will, but the Spirit of God does.

The Holy Spirit will make an unwilling sinner willing to take the Gospel or to learn more and more about the Gospel and make him run to the cross at the feet of Christ. The Holy Spirit will make people who have laughed at Jesus and Christians to ask Christ for mercy.

The unbeliever will be willing to believe through the power of the Holy Spirit. The unbeliever will gladly rejoice at the sound of the name of Jesus through the power of the Holy Spirit. He is very, very delighted to obey God's commandments and read God's Word.

He is ready to be the doer of God's Word in every area of his life. The Holy Spirit of God is the only one who has the power to change the will of men and women.

Many Christian are not complete in Christ their hearts are partially impure, they lust in all kinds of sexual immoralities, they exercise greed and evil thoughts. We have to rejoice because Christ is our hope of the glory.

A day will come it will not be long, that God will complete what He started in the lives of men and women. He will present believers as a perfect bride to the bridegroom Jesus, perfect in the Spirit with no blemishes or spots, presented at the feet of God without impurities or contamination.

Believers will be able to say on that great day that glory is our God. We have been cleansed through the blood of Jesus; through the work of the Holy Spirit we are clean.

Believers must praise the power of the Holy Spirit for making us fit to stand before the throne of Grace, before our Father in heaven through the love and mercy of God. The power of the Holy Spirit will continue to pour out to unbelievers and sinners. The Holy Spirit will continue to pour out again in a wonderful way that will go everywhere to increase knowledge and understanding of the Lord on earth, just as water fills the sea.

# 6

# The Introduction of the Fruit of the Spirit

The Fruit of the Spirit is: love, joy, peace, patience, kindness, goodness, faithfulness, gentleness, self- control, obedience, meekness, humbleness, truth, righteousness, forgiveness, longsuffering, forbearance, temperance, and self-esteem.

Of all of the fruits of the Spirit, Apostle Paul made nine of them the visible attributes of true Christian life, according to Gal. 5:22. These fruits of the Spirit characterize all who are truly walking in the power of the Holy Spirit.

These are the fruits that all Christians should be producing in a new life with Jesus Christ our Lord and Savior. They are a physical manifestation of a Christian's transformed life. "Being filled with all unrighteousness, fornication, wickedness, covetousness, maliciousness; full of envy, murder, debate, deceit, malignity; whisperers. Backbiters, haters of God, spiteful, proud, boasters, inventors of evil things disobedient to parents. Without understanding, covenant breakers, without natural affection implacable, unmerciful." Rom. 1:29-31.

"Let us walk honestly, as in the day; not in rioting and drunkenness, not in chambering and wantonness, not in strife and envying." Rom. 13:13.

"But brother goeth to law with brother and that before the unbelievers. Now therefore there is utterly a fault among you, because ye go to law one with another. Why do ye not rather take wrong?

Why do ye not rather suffer yourselves to be defrauded? and that your brethren. Know ye not that the unrighteous shall not inherit the kingdom of God? Be not deceived: neither fornicators, nor idolaters, nor adulterers, nor effeminate, nor abusers of themselves with mankind.

Nor thieves, nor covetous, nor drunkards, nor revilers, nor extortioners, shall inherit the kingdom of God." 1 Cor. 6:6-10.

"For I fear, lest when I come, I shall not find you such as I would, and that I shall be found unto you such as you would not: lest there be debates, envying, wraths, strifes, back-biting, whisperings, swellings, tumults."

2 Cor. 12:20. Wicked people will not inherit the kingdom of God. For example, some Corinthians, during the time of Apostle Paul, believed that they could

end their relationship and fellowship with Christ, live immoral and unjust lives, and that their salvation and inheritance in God's kingdom would still be secured.

Paul made clear to them that spiritual death is the consequence of continuously sinning against God. The same applies to all Believers in Christ today nothing has changed. This direct warning applies to the entire Christian community, wherever they may be all over the world. Believers must live a clean pure life.

"Now the works of the flesh are manifest, which are these; Adultery, fornication, uncleanness, lasciviousness. Idolatry, witchcraft, hated, variance, emulations, wrath, strife seditions, heresies, envying, murders, drunkenness. I tell you before as I have also told you in time past, that they which do such things shall not inherit the kingdom of God." Gal. 5:19-21.

Paul made these traits clear and maintained that it is impossible to inherit the kingdom of God by observing the law, as well as that it is impossible to close the door to the kingdom of heaven because one engages in the immoral and evil practices that are going on in the world. "But the fruit of the spirit is love, joy peace, longsuffering, gentleness, goodness, faith. Meekness, temperance, against such there is no law." Gal. 5:22-23.

A true believer of Jesus Christ must produce fruit for righteousness and be obedient to the word and the commandment of God through the Power of the Holy Spirit that indwells us.

"Finally, brethren, whatsoever things are true, whatsoever things are honest, whatsoever things are just, whatsoever things are pure, whatsoever things are lovely, whatsoever things are good report, if there be any virtue, and if there be any praise, think on these things." Php. 4:8.

# 7

# The Fruit of the Spirit: LOVE

" Though I speak with the tongues of men and of angels, and have not charity, I am become as sounding brass, or a tinkling cymbal. And now abideth faith, hope, and charity, these three; but the greatest of these is charity." 1 Cor. 13:1, 13.

These two verses reveal the biblical meaning of Love's supreme importance to life. Apostle Paul, in his letter to the Corinthian Church, concluded that love will never end; love will always be of use.

The gift we receive from God is bestowed with the love of God. God's gifts of the fruit of the Holy Spirit are given with power to enhance believers' ability to serve God in various areas of the Church. The need for love is never-ending; it never becomes absolute.

God wants us to use love on every occasion, everywhere. Love is something we grow in. It must be perfected. God gave us love; He showers His love upon us, as we need it every day. We must see ourselves as mature believers of Jesus Christ. A time is coming when love will be perfected; we will have abundant love for one another as children of God. Believers must pursue love as long as we are still in the flesh. The love of

God comes through the actions of God through His Spirit, something supernatural. "And hope maketh not ashamed; because the love of God is shed abroad in our hearts by the Holy Ghost which is given unto us." Rom. 5:5.

Christians experience the love of God. God's love for believers is in their hearts through the Holy Spirit, especially in times of trouble. The Spirit of God continues to flood our hearts with the love of God and the full presence of God in order to sustain us through any problems and circumstances.

God is the source of love; His love abides in us forever. Apostle John said, "Beloved, let us love one another: for love is of God; and every one that loveth is born of God, and knoweth God. He that loveth not knoweth not God; for God is love.

"In this was manifested the love of God toward us, and sent His Son to be the propitiation for our sins. Beloved, if God so loved us, we ought also to love one another. No man hath seen God at any time. If we love one another, God dwell in us, and His love perfected in us." 1 John 4:7-12.

Love is an aspect of the fruit of the Holy Spirit and the evidence of new birth. It is also something that we are responsible for developing as believers in Jesus Christ. Apostle John exhorts us to love one another; he wants us to be concerned with them and look out for the welfare of the sick and the needy among us.

If we are pursuing a Christ-like character, these verses are very important to all believers in Jesus Christ because they tell us so much about God and our responsibilities. This verse explains to us that love is of God, that He is the source of love.

Apostle John explained that the true love of God normally becomes a part of man's nature. God is a living, dynamic, and powerful force in our lives. Every activity of God is love. Love can be seen in every activity of God. God creates the universe with love; God rules all the earth in love.

God judges all the nations of the earth in love. Everything that God does expresses His nature. God and His nature are manifested by everything that He does. By God's love, He was revealed and known. Love reveals God to man.

The existence of life in others besides Him is an act of love. God's love is revealed in His providence and care for His creations. God's love is the evidence of redemption and our hope for eternal life. God made us in His own image and likeness.

"But the hour cometh, and now is, when the true worshippers shall worship the Father in spirit and in truth: for the Father seeketh such to worship him. God is a Spirit: and they that worship Him must worship Him in spirit and in truth." John 4:23-24.

Our Lord teaches that true worship must come to God with complete sincerity and with a spirit that is directed by the life and activity of the Holy Spirit. Therefore, our worship must take place according to the truth of the Father that is revealed in the Son and received through the Spirit.

Jesus explained to the people of His days that those who worship and have set aside the truth of the doctrine of the Word of God have also set aside the only foundation for true worship. This means that we cannot express true love without the power of the Spirit of God that indwells all believers.

We cannot be what God wants us to be until we have the fruit of love that the Holy Spirit provides. All believers must love with the love of God in their lives. Jesus Christ teaches that, "God is a Spirit." "In Spirit" means the level at which true worship occurs.

Believers must come to God with complete sincerity and with a Spirit that is directed by the life and activities of the Holy Spirit. Truth is a characteristic of God incarnate in Christ, intrinsic to the Holy Spirit, and at the heart of the Gospel. Therefore, worship must take place in accordance with the truth of the Father that is revealed in the Son and received through the Holy Spirit.

Sacrifice is another vital part of God's love. God's love was manifest in His Son and is perfected in His people. God's love is perfected in the lives of all his children. We believers reproduce God's love among ourselves and the love of God flows through us to non-believers.

God is concerned about our blessing as well as about our perfection of his love in the lives of the saints of God. We can love according to God's love when we get closer to Him and do what is pleasing in His eyes. Believers must learn how to love God; we must follow his commandments, and maintain fellowship and an intimate relationship with him. God is love.

He forgives us for all of our trespasses and sin through His Son Jesus Christ, and He is the sustainer of the universe and everything that is in it. The Bible says, "Whosoever believeth that Jesus is the Christ is born of God; and everyone that loveth Him that begat loveth him also that is begotten of him.

"By this we know that we love the children of God, when we love God, and keep His commandments. For this is the love of God, that we keep his commandments: and His commandments are not grievous." 1 John 5:1-3.

Genuine faith will express itself in gratitude to and for the love of the Father and Jesus Christ His Son.

Faith and love are inseparable, for when we are born of God, the Holy Spirit pours the love of God into our hearts. Love for others is the second greatest commandment for genuine Christians. Love is accompanied by love for God. Our Lord Jesus Christ stated that we should love the Lord our God and love our neighbor.

All believers must be obedient to Christ's commandments. The commandments of God are clean. The basic elements of love include what direction actions should take for us to show love. This means that obedience to God is the only means of proving our love to Him.

Obedience constitutes action submitting to God's commandments, principles revealed in His word, and examples of God or the godly. We must know that this is where godly love is in human beings. Obeying God's commands is love because God is love; His very nature is Love. It is impossible for Him not to love us.

He loved us before the foundation of the world. He gives us commandments in love, which will produce right and good results. Our Lord said, "If you love me, keep my commandments." John 14:15.

Keeping God's commandments is how we express our love for him. "If ye keep my commandments, ye shall abide in my love, even as I have kept my Father's commandments, and abide in His love." John 15:10.

Jesus Christ calls us to a life of holy intimacy and personal devotion to Him. This is possible because of

God's love for us, which He has poured into our hearts through the Holy Spirit. God the Father Almighty demonstrated His great love through Christ's death and resurrection, while we were still sinners.

We must remain in Jesus' love by pursuing spiritual intimacy and communion with Him, and by obeying His commandments just as He came to this world and obeyed His Father's commandments throughout His earthly ministry. By this we know that we know Him if we keep His commandments.

Love is the fruit, the product of the Spirit, which is now developing in our lives. The Holy Spirit guides believers and leads them to the truth. It is the responsibility of the believer to follow the Spirit's guidance and to obey the truths of God who created us in His own image.

Obedience to His commandments is godly love; the fruit of the Spirit empowers believers with the goodness of the Almighty Creator. Each aspect of the fruit listed here is simply a reflection of God's character, reproduced in us by His Spirit. "By this shall all men know that ye are my disciples, if ye have love for one another." John 13:35.

Christ is telling us that love must be the distinguishing mark of His disciples and of all believers—love that is self-giving and sacrificial, and that seeks good for others. This means that the relationship among all believers must be characterized by devotion and concern, sacrificially seeking the highest good of their brothers and sisters in Christ.

Christians must be sensitive to each other's feelings and reputation, and sometimes deny themselves in order to help other believers in Christ. The Holy Spirit has poured out God's love in our hearts. "And hope maketh not ashamed; because the love of God is shed abroad in our hearts by the Holy Ghost which is given unto us." Rom. 5:5.

"He that loveth not knoweth not God; for God is love." 1 John 4:8. Love is the foundation of His character. Apostle

Paul said, "Charity suffereth long, and is kind; charity envieth not; charity vaunteth not itself, is not puffed up, doth not behave itself unseemly, seeketh not her own, is not easily provoked, thinketh no evil." 1 Cor. 13:4-5.

This shows that every phase of the fruit of the Spirit is merely a specific expression of godly love. Love is an activity and manner, not just inner feelings or motivation. The various phases of love included here characterize God the Father, the Son and the Holy Spirit.

Every believer must seek to grow in this model of love. Jesus teaches us that we should not only love our friends and relatives, but we must also love our enemies. Our Lord again emphasizes our need for extra help from God the Holy Spirit. Our Lord said that we should not return evil for evil, but rather return evil with good.

Love expresses a desire that everyone in the universe holds. People sometimes think about love or see it as a sense of regard, a strong desire, to be satisfied by caring for one another. People of this earth express their love in so many ways that other people cannot imagine.

While a measure of caring for one another can be true love, caring by itself is not love. "And now abideth faith, hope, charity, these three; but the greatest of these is charity." 1 Cor. 13:13.

This verse reveals love's supreme value of love, faith, hope, prophecy, sacrifice, knowledge, and the gift of speaking in tongues. God gave believers all these gifts in order to serve Him in all areas of Church ministries.

Believers received the gifts of God with the Holy Spirit's power to enhance us in order to function in the Church's ministries and to be able to live fruitful lives as Christians. If any fruits of the Spirit are not use with love, this will not be what God wants for believers.

"Knowledge puffeth up, but charity edifieth means love builds up." Paul explained to believers that pride has the power to ruin the knowledge of a child of God. Our knowledge could be corrupted if the believer does not apply it with love. This is the main reason why Paul compares the gift of God with love to inform us of and to strongly emphasize the importance of love. Love is more important and is very valuable in the lives of the children of God.

If any believer does not have love, that person is not complete in Christ. The love of God always comes through the power of God in the Holy Spirit. Love is the fulfillment of the law.

Paul emphasizes love by telling us that we should submit to and honor government as God's chosen people managing human affairs. All Christians must follow government rules and regulations.

Love can motivate us to follow the law of the country we live in, which shows God's commandment that says if a believer exercises God's love in his or her life, he will also follow the ten commandments without breaking them.

Love motivates and its presence is needed in all we do in our daily lives, whether we are believers or non-believers. Another important aspect of love appears in our community and in our Church. The fruit of the Spirit should be known, revered, and manifested in the lives of all Christians.

This fruit characterizes all who truly walk in the Holy Spirit; these are the fruits that all Christians should produce in their new lives with Jesus Christ. Believers must be able to understand each of the fruits of the Spirit. "And we have known and believed the love that God hath to us. God is love; and he that dwelleth in love dwelleth in God, and God in him." 1John 4:16.

God is love. Whoever lives in love lives in God and God in him, so we know and rely on the love God has for us. Love is through Jesus Christ. Our greatest goal is to live and do all things in love, to show love wherever we are, in whatever we are doing, and to do so with the love of God that he has shed in our hearts.

Love is the act of applying love everywhere, in every place, in everything, at all times, every hour, every minute and every moment. 1 Cor. 13:4-8. The fruit of the Spirit is very important for all Christians, whether infants in Christ or Christians with the solid food of the Word of God.

We are all in need of the fruit of the Spirit. Love is the first fruit of the Spirit, for a very good reason, because it was out of the love of God that man was created. God created human beings in His own image and He continually reaches out to human beings despite our behavior, as we are continuously running away from Him.

God's love for us made Him sacrifice His only begotten Son in order to save us from our Sin. Jesus Christ came to this world to save the sinners, the lost, the unbelievers, and the idol-worshipers. Christ preached the Gospel of God for good three years out of His love for us.

Christ shows His love to us when he was about to ascend to heaven, by giving a great commission to all of the apostles and believers after them, to "Go ye and preach, teach the Gospel in all the nations so that human beings will be saved from their past, present, and future sins."

This fruit of the Spirit's love comes in so many forms; the fruit of the Spirit's love is unconditional love. It is the love of a mother and child, where the mother has given her life in order to save the life of her baby. This is the reason it is listed first.

This is why Apostle Paul emphasizes that love is very important—it is the completeness, permanence, and supremacy over all mechanisms of the sustainer of human life. "I am the true vine, and my Father is the husbandman." John 15:1.

Here, Our Lord Jesus describes Himself as the true vine and His disciples and all believers as the branches. Our main goal is to remain attached to Him as the source of our life in order to produce fruit. God the Father is the gardener who takes care of the branches in order that they may bear fruit and more fruit.

God expects all believers to bear fruit. Our Lord Jesus stated, "Herein is my Father glorified, that ye bear much fruit; so shall ye be my disciples." John 15: 8. All Christians must exhibit the likeness of Christ to the world; we must let our light shine in order to glorify our Father in heaven. We imitate

Christ everywhere we are and prove that we are part of His body. He mentions fruit with regard to His commandments. "Ye have not chosen me. But I have chosen you and ordained you, that ye should go and bring forth fruit, and that your fruit should remain: that whatsoever ye shall ask of the Father in my name, He may give it you." John 15:16.

Christ made it clear that He was the one who chose every believer for salvation and eternal life. He chose us for discipleship and fruitfulness as missionaries and pastors, and for ordaining ministers and teachers of the Word of God. He chose for all Christians to go into the world to bear fruit.

To bear the fruits of Love, Joy, Peace, etc., and for doing our best to convert souls into His Holy hands. This instruction of our Lord shows clearly that a believer must live the life of a fruit-bearer.

Bearing fruit is generalized, clear, and precise; bearing fruit includes everything produced as a result of their labors of publicly preaching the Gospel, their service to the Church in pasturing, in all their ministry work, and their personal triumphs and growth in God's image.

The fruits of the Spirit are produced by the action of the Holy Spirit in us. "But if ye be led of the Spirit, ye are not under the law." Rom. 8:14. Not all believers in Jesus Christ are under the law because they are led by the Spirit of God.

To be led by the Spirit means to be lifted above the flesh and to be occupied with the Lord. When the Spirit of God fills us, we have no room to think of the law of the flesh. The Spirit of God will not lead believers in Christ to look at the law of the flesh; He will point believers to Christ as the only ground of acceptance before God.

Being led by the Spirit is a characteristic of all Christians. The Spirit of Christ indwelling us will resist the motion and any thought of evil in the heart of the believer. "Howbeit when he, the Spirit of truth, is come, he will guide you into all truth: for he shall not speak of himself; but whatsoever he shall hear, that shall he speak: and he will shew you things to come." John 16:13.

Our Lord says, however, when it, the Spirit of Truth, has come, It will guide you into all truth, for it will not speak on its own authority. Rather, whatever it hears, it will speak and it will tell you things to come.

The Holy Spirit allows us to choose voluntarily and consciously to submit to the Word of God. The power of God the Holy Spirit is described generally as the Power of God, which is correct, but power comes in a number of forms.

God loves us, Jesus Christ is the Word of God, and the Bible is the written revelation of God that was written because God is concerned about our minds and what we put in our minds, because whatever goes into our minds produces the fruit of our lives.

"And you hath he quickened, who were dead in trespasses and sins; Wherein time past ye walked according to the course of this world, according to the prince of the power of the air, the spirit that now worketh in the children of disobedience: Among whom also we all had our conversation in times past in the lusts of our flesh, fulfilling the desires of the flesh and of the mind; and were by nature the children of wrath, even as others." Eph. 2:1-3.

He made us alive. We were dead in our trespasses and sins, in which we walked according to the course of this world and according to the prince of the power of the air, the spirit who drives the sons and daughters to waywardness, where we once conducted ourselves in the lust of flesh, fulfilling the desires of the flesh and of the mind, doing things not approved of by God.

This is the reason that, after our conversion, God the Holy Spirit indwelled us and planted the fruit of the Spirit of God in us. "Now we have received, not the Spirit of the world, but the Spirit which is of God; that we might know the things that have been freely given to us by God." 1 Cor. 2:12.

Christ's blood enables us to have access to a new and infinitely larger and more beautiful life, beyond what we can imagine. We now possess good fruit in our minds and produce the fruit of the Spirit of God. We became a Spirit-filled believer.

"These things we also speak, not, in words which man's wisdom teaches but which the Holy Spirit teaches, comparing Spiritual things with spiritual but the natural man does not receive the things of the

Spirit of God, for they are foolishness to him; nor can he know them, because they are spiritually discerned." 1 Cor. 2: 13-14.

Love is one of the most important and fundamental concepts in the New Testament; love is a divine attribute. "For God so love the world." John 3:16. "We know love by this that He laid down His life for us." John 13:35.

This is best expressed by Christians' love within the body of Christ. The last aspect of God's love mentioned is a very important one of the Christian experience.

"Beloved, let us love one another, for love is from God; and everyone who loves is born of God and knows God. The one who does not love does not know God, for God is love." John 4:7-8.

Covenant love means the love of God that stands behind, stands in, and stands through His redemption, the redemptive work of Jesus Christ. It is a love that was born in the heart of God for lost humanity, and revealed to humanity in the redemptive work of Christ throughout the history of the universe.

It is God's love that sends Jesus into the world as an offering for our sins, a love incarnated in His Son Jesus Christ, and a love that is also incarnated in the lives of Christ's disciples and all believers in Christ until the end of ages.

All Christians are called to model and manifest Christ's love in their lives and to walk in love as he walked in their lives; believers must transfer the love of Christ in them to non- believers around them. Our Lord said, "Let your light so shine before men, that they may see your good works, and glorify your Father which is in heaven." Matt. 5:16.

Believers must love as Christ loves, they must be givers, giving to those who are in need and those who ask for help from them. "For God so loved the world that he gave his only begotten Son, that whosoever believeth in him should not perish, but have everlasting life." Rom. 8:16.

This verse reveals the heart and purpose of God. God's love is so big that it embraces all people on earth. God gave His son as an offering for sin on the cross. This atonement proceeds from the loving heart of God.

It was not something that anyone could force on anybody else. There are three aspects of believing in the Gospel of God. This includes the sure conviction that Jesus Christ is the Son of God and the only Savior for lost humanity.

Surrender to His lordship and fellowship with a heart obedient to Christ and with full assurance of trust in the Lord Jesus Christ. He is both able and willing to bring you to salvation and to fellowship with God the Father in heaven.

This love was manifested in Jesus when He gave, "And walk in love, as Christ also hath loved us, and hath given Himself for us, as an offering and a sacrifice to God a sweet smelling savor." Eph. 5:2.

This is the love of self-giving. It is a mysterious incarnation that affirms that God, who gave His Son, is also God who gave Himself. "To wit, that God was in Christ, reconciling the world unto himself, not imputing their trespasses unto them; and hath committed unto us the word of reconciliation." 2 Cor. 5:19.

Reconciliation is one important aspect of Christ's work of redemption the restoration of the sinner to fellowship with God the Father. Through Christ's atoning death, God has removed the barrier of sin and has opened a way for the sinner to return to fellowship with Him.

Reconciliation becomes effective for each believer through his or her personal confession of sins, repentance, and faith in Christ. Christ models the same self-given love through His crucifixion, His death on the cross.

Jesus Christ's sacrificial love was not only in the Old Testament as atonement, but in the sense of giving Himself for the life of people in the world. "Greater love hath no man than this that man lay down his life for his friends." John 15:13.

God's love is an intimate love; believers maintain personal and intimate love with God through the power of the indwelling of the Holy Spirit. Christ showed intimate love during His earthly ministry. He visits Mary and Martha and ministered to them in their home. Another aspect of the love of God is Jesus' unconditional love for believers all over the world. God's love stands steadfast, "We love Him because he love us first." Jn. 4:19.

"But God commendeth His own love towards us, in that while we were yet sinners, Christ died for us." Rom. 5:8. This type of love involves complete acceptance of Christ. It also involves unlimited forgiveness, just as Christ forgave our sins. "Forbearing one another and forgiving one another, if any man has a quarrel against any: even as Christ forgave you, so also do ye." Col. 3:13.

The example of Christ's unlimited forgiveness was heard on the cross when He said, "Father, forgive them; for they know not what they do." Luke 23:34. Our Lord's first word on the cross was forgiving this shows His unlimited love for human beings and all His creations.

Believers must love as God loves, meaning loving vulnerably, unselfishly, and intimately, and having unconditional love for others. It poses the risk of being exploited, taking advantage of oneself, misunderstanding, and abuse.

It is a love that exposes the believer continuously to rejection, hurt, and persecution. Jesus Christ was rejected by people of His days, like the Pharisees, Sadducees, and all other people including some women when He was on the cross. "He came unto His own, and His own received Him not." John 1:11.

He was even misunderstood by his mother, brother, sister, and friends. The light of Christ shines in an evil and sinful world. The majority of the people in the world do not accept the life and light of Jesus.

Christ illuminates all who hear His Gospel by imparting a measure of grace and understanding, so that they may freely choose to accept or reject the Gospel, in order for them to be saved.

The people of the world means unbelievers who will never recognize Jesus they will remain as enemies of Christ and His gospel until the end of the age when Christ returns. Jesus Christ's love is enduring and everlasting.

God's love is steadfast and enduring for His children; God's love followed the Israelites from the Old Testament through the wilderness for forty years in the wilderness. "I have spread out my hands all the day unto a rebellious people, which walketh in a way that was not good, after their own thoughts." Isa. 65:2.

God responds to the prophet Isaiah's prayer by describing His continuous appeal to the rebellious nation to return to Him. God tells them to repent; otherwise, He will repay them with His judgment. God the Father transferred the same love to Jesus. Today, Jesus Christ's love continues in our lives and He continues to call us to repent and come back to the Father.

"Looking unto Jesus the author and finisher of our faith; who for the joy that was set before him endured the cross, despising the shame, and is set down at the right hand of the throne of God." Heb. 12:2.

The goal of believers' is faith; we should look to Jesus, focus all of our attention on Him, trust Him, and commit to His will for us. Believers will overcome temptation through prayer and by seeking the joy of completing the work that the Father calls us to do for His great glory.

Believers need to fix their eyes on Jesus at all times the author and finisher of our faith. The cross and life of Jesus were characteristic of humbleness and obedience to God the Father. Christ's obedience to the Father began at His incarnation.

He came to this world in our own form, "but made Himself of no reputation, and took upon him the form of a servant, and was made in the likeness of men. And being found in fashion as a man, he humbled himself, and became obedient unto death, even the death of the cross." Php. 2.7-8.

Christ voluntarily emptied Himself through love, His heavenly glory, His position, eternal riches, and the use of His divine powers. The main importance of His emptiness is the acceptance of human limitations, suffering, misunderstanding, ill treatment, hatred, and the curse of death on the cross.

Christ fully retained His divine nature; He also took on a fully human nature, with it temptations, humiliations, and weaknesses, yet without sin. "For consider Him that endured such contradiction of sinners against Himself, lest ye be wearied and faint in your minds." Heb. 12:3.

The love that sent Jesus Christ to the cross for us sinners is an enduring love. Let all believers, with their love for Christ, endure persecution in order to win souls for Christ. Love is the fruit of the Spirit; it is the result of sound soul fruit, and it is the fruit that the Holy Spirit produces for all the believers.

Every Believer must bear fruit in his or her own life, more and more fruit; so that he or she can clearly see God's sacrificial, self-giving love, which is incomprehensible, "And hope maketh not ashamed; because the love of God is shed abroad in our hearts by the Holy Ghost which is given unto us." Rom. 5:5.

God has poured out His love into the believer's entire heart. The love of God poured out in the believer's heart through the Holy Spirit is always greater than faith, hope, or anything in this world.

Christians experience the love of God in their hearts through the power of the Holy Spirit, especially in times of trouble. The Spirit of God continues to flood believers' hearts with love.

It is this ever-present experience of God's love that sustains believers in suffering and assures them that their hope for future glory is not misleading. Christ is coming back—this is very certain. Through the Spirit's life and power, we can possess and express a truly intimate, unconditional, and enduring love. God is always at work in us, "For it is God which worketh in you both to will and to do of His good pleasure." Php. 2:13.

God's grace works in His children to produce in them both the desire and power to do His will. God's work is not one of compulsion or irresistible grace. The work of grace within us is always dependent on our cooperation and response of faith in the Holy Spirit.

All believers in Jesus Christ must strive to bear the first fruit of the Spirit's love, which God himself demonstrated from the beginning of the creation of the world and in the lives of individuals through believers and non-believers. The Holy Spirit energizes the growth of the fruit of the spiritual lives of believers.

It is very important that Apostle Paul explained the difference between the works of the flesh and the fruit of the Spirit. The fruit is like a grown tree and the branches abiding in the vine. The Holy Spirit produces one kind of fruit, which is Christ's likeness.

All the fruit of the Spirit that was listed describes the characteristics of the children of God. Love is what God is, and that is what the entire body of Christ must be, while Joy is Christians' contentment and satisfaction with God and with His operations in believers' lives.

"Now these three remain: faith, hope and love, but the greatest of these is love."1 Cor. 13:13. Apostle Paul made it clear that God exalts Christ-like character more than ministerial work, faith, or the possession of spiritual gifts.

God values and emphasizes the character that acts in love, patience, kindness, unselfishness, honesty, endurance, and righteousness more than faith and great achievement in the ministerial work. The more important people in God's kingdom will be those who display genuine love for God and for people.

Love in Greek is called *"agape,"* which all Christians refer to and call unconditional love. Agape love means an undefeatable benevolence and unconquerable goodwill of believers in God that always seeks the highest in others, no matter what he or she does or is doing or is about to do.

It is the self-giving love that gives freely without asking anything in return, and does not consider the price of its object. Agape love is not a love by choice; it means love by chance, and it refers to the will rather than emotion. Agape-love explains the unconditional love of God for the universe; agape love is a sacrificial love, demonstrated by Jesus Christ on the cross at the Calvary.

"Love endures long and is patient and kind, love never is envious nor boils over with jealousy, is not boastful or vainglorious, does not display itself haughtily. It is not conceited, not arrogant and proud; it is not rude and does not act unbecomingly.

"Love does not insist on its own rights or its own way, for it is not self-seeking; it is not touchy or fretful or resentful; it takes no account of the evil done to it, it pays no attention to a suffered wrong.

"Love does not rejoice at injustice and unrighteousness, but rejoices when right and truth prevail.

"Love bears up under anything and every things that comes, is ever ready to believe the best of every person, its hopes are fadeless under circumstances, and it endures everything without weakening love never fades out or becomes obsolete or come to an end. Love never fails." 1 Cor. 13:4-8. (Taken from the NIV New Believers' Bible Commentary.)

The second demonstration of the Holy Spirit's power was the resurrection of Jesus, "when He raised him from the dead." Eph. 1:20. Jesus Christ was raised by the power of the Holy Spirit. Jesus was raised by the Father. The resurrection of Jesus Christ was attributed to God the Father. "Him hath God exalted with his right hand to be Prince and Saviour for to give repentance to Israel, and forgiveness of sins." Acts 5:31.

"And the angel answered and said unto her. The Holy Ghost shall come upon three, and the power of the Highest shall overshadow thee: therefore also that holy thing which shall be born of thee shall be called the Son of God." Luke 1:35.

"But if the Spirit of him that raised up Jesus from the dead dwell in you, he that raised up Jesus from the dead dwell in you, shall also quicken your mortal bodies by his Spirit that dwelleth in you." Rom. 8:11.

The resurrection of Jesus Christ was achieved by the power of the Holy Spirit. When they brought Christ down from the cross and His mother Mary held him on her legs and found out that He was completely dead, she lifted Him up.

His eyes were closed, His hands; she checked His side where the sword had pierced, the sword that the Roman solder struck on Him in order to be sure that He was dead. She saw the nails in his hands and legs, and found out that Christ was completely dead.

Everybody was surprised including Nicodemus, who was there to help Joseph, Arimathea, and all of the Apostles. He was put inside the grave and the stone was rolled to cover the grave. All life was gone on the third day He was raised up through the power of the Holy Spirit.

The illumination power of the Holy Spirit descend into the grave and came upon Jesus, shine upon His lifeless body, just as God spoke to prophet Ezekiel: "And he said unto me, son of man, can these bones live? And I answered, 'O Lord God, thou knowest.' And again he said unto me, 'Prophesy upon these bones, and say unto them, O ye dry bones, hear the word of the Lord.

Thus saith the Lord God unto these bones'; Behold, I will cause breath to enter into you, and ye shall live." Eze. 37:3-5.

Christ was made brand new; He arose. The angels rolled the stone away from the grave's entrance. When the Roman guards saw what happened and saw Jesus walking out of the tomb, they were terrified and ran away. Christ arose; death had no more dominion over Him. He conquered death forever and forever.

He arose, Halleluiah. Christ arose the blessed Ruler of the souls of all human lives forever more. "For Christ also hath once suffered for sins, the just for the unjust, that He might bring us to God, being put to death in the flesh, but quickened by the Spirit." 1 Pet. 3:18.

We see the power of the Holy Spirit in the work of grace; by His grace we are saved. "Not by works of righteousness which we have done, but according to his mercy he saved us, by washing of regeneration, and renewing of the Holy Ghost." Titus 3:5.

The power of the Spirit is the inner spiritual power of the Holy Spirit. The inner power of the Holy Spirit has power over men and women, including non-believers. The work and power of the Holy Spirit will continue until Christ's return onto this earth.

The Spirit of God holds this earth; He is the sustainer of this universe. If the Spirit of God should leave this earth today, this earth will perish. We thank

God for His unfailing love towards us in this universe; His Spirit will not leave until Christ returns to judge the quick and the dead, and all the eyes shall see Him.

# 8

# The Fruit of the Spirit: JOY

It is very important to know that joy is produced by divine origin, which is God. This means that joy is not a human-based happiness that comes and goes; rather, joy came and originated from God.

It takes a whole heart given to God to totally and fully obey the commandments of God without the helper, the Holy Spirit, who proceeds from the Father and the Son. Whatever our position, hard times, and sorrow, we can still have joy, because He gave us His Spirit.

The fruit of the Spirit of God produces fruits in us every day that help us in any tribulations, afflictions persecutions, rejections and all the things that are happening in this world that we don't understand and that are very hard to bear and comprehend, unbearable situations.

"Behold, thou desire truth in the inward parts; and in the hidden part thou shall make one to know wisdom. Purge me with hyssop, and I shall be clean; wash me, and I shall be whiter than snow. Make me to hear joy and gladness; that the bones which thou has broken many rejoice. Hide thy face from my sins, and blot out all mine iniquities." Psl. 51:6-10.

"For his anger endureth but a moment; in his favor is life: weeping may endure for a night, but joy cometh in the morning." Psl. 30:5.

Another example of joy is that of Apostle Paul and Silas—both of them were thrown into prison and their feet fastened in the stocks. "Who, having received such a charge, thrust them into the inner prison, and made their feet fast in the stocks." Acts 16:24-25.

At midnight, the Spirit of God showered his blessings on them from above and they were full of joy that they had never experienced before in their lives; they began to pray and sing songs of praise to the Lord.

The prisoners heard them singing and they joined them in their singing. They sang songs of praise to the Lord because they were very happy in the middle of their circumstances. They trusted in the Lord, and they put their hope in him.

Their songs of praise reached heaven. The gate of the prison opened but they all stayed there; nobody ran away. This action of Paul and Silas made the Jailer ask them, "What do I need to do to be saved?" Acts 16:30.

The Apostles responded to him: believe in the Lord Jesus Christ. To believe in the Lord Jesus is to focus our faith and commitment on the person of Christ. He is our redeemer from sin, our Savior from damnation, and the Lord of our lives.

Believers must totally trust Him. He is the true Son of God sent by the Father and all authority has been given unto Him in heaven and on this earth. The jailer was saved together with his entire family.

Another example of joy is that of Job's sickness and afflictions on all his family, despite which, he never stopped trusting in the Lord. "And the Lord turned the captivity of Job, when he prayed for his friends: also the Lord gave Job twice as much as he had before." Job 42:10.

God gave His children many reasons to have joy in our lives, no matter what trials we are facing. Paul's thorn in the flesh did not stop his joy in the Lord: "My grace is sufficient for thee; for my strength is made perfect in weakness." 2 Cor. 12:9-10.

Paul replied and said, "Most gladly therefore, will I rather glory in my infirmities, that the power of Christ may rest upon me. Therefore I take pleasure in infirmities, in reproaches, in necessities, in persecutions, in distresses for Christ sake: For when I am weak, then am I strong." 2 Cor. 12:10.

We need the power and strength of God in our lives as believers in Jesus Christ. The grace of God abounds more and more everyday in our lives. Grace is the presence, favor, and power of God through the Holy Spirit. God's grace and power are most clearly seen and profoundly revealed in the midst of our human weaknesses.

The greater our weakness and trials for Christ, the more the grace of God will help us to accomplish His will. What God gives is always sufficient for us to live our daily lives, to work for him, and to endure our suffering.

As long as we draw near and get close to Jesus Christ, He will give us His heavenly strength and comfort. We will be able to see eternal values in our weaknesses, for it is Christ's power that rests upon us and lives within us as we walk through life towards our heavenly dwelling.

Paul and Job knew that God had a plan for their lives. Since they belonged to him, they were ready to suffer so that sinners could be saved. The birth of our Lord Jesus brought great joy to the world and the angel sang and said to them, "And the angel said unto them, fear not: for, behold, I bring you good tidings of great joy, which shall be to all the people. For unto you a child is born this day in the city of David a savior, which is Christ the Lord." Luke 2:10-11.

The life of Jesus on earth brings joy to those who believe in Him and followed Him during His earthly ministry. He healed the sick, preached, and taught the gospel of God. He performed many miracles: lame people walked, the blind received their sight, the dead were raised to life, the sick were completely made whole, the salvation of God was spread from Capernaum, Jericho, Bethlehem, Nazareth, Jerusalem, Galilee, and throughout the sea of Tiberea, Ganazarette and to the Garden of Gethsemane.

Our Lord brings joy to people wherever He goes: to the home of Matthew and Mary, to the home of Zaccheaus, to the home of Peter's mother- in-law, to the home of Matthew, to Mary-Magdalene, and to Matius, the son of Timeaus on the road to Jericho.

He brought joy to the man who was born blind, the man at the Bethsaida of thirty-eight years of infirmities, to the woman who was bent and could not walk right or see the sky, and to the man with the withered hand. He brought joy to five thousand men, not including women and children, by feeding them.

They were so full that the same joy extended and spread to the poor who did not have the means or opportunity to be there, but received the twelve baskets of leftovers. He also brought joy to four thousand people, with seven baskets of leftovers for the poor and needy.

Joy was brought to Malchus, one of the soldiers whose ear Peter cut on the night of Jesus' arrest; Jesus restored the man's ear back. Our Lord brought joy to the thief on His right hand by inviting him to meet

Him in paradise, on the night of His crucifixion. Jesus Christ brought great joy to the two people on Emmaus Road when He opened the Scripture for them; their hearts burned with joy as they ran back to the Apostles and told them that our risen Lord had spoken to them.

"And they said one to another, did not our heart burn within us, while he talked with us by the way, and while he opened to us the scriptures?" Luke 24:32.

He has risen indeed. Jesus brought great joy to the Jewish and the Gentiles because of His sacrifice on the cross in order to bring salvation to sinners and the lost, as well as unbelievers all over the world.

Jesus brought great joy to all who believed in Him and his gift of grace, eternal life, and everlasting life. "For God so love the world, that he gave his only begotten Son, that whosoever believeth in him should not perish, but has everlasting live." John 3:16.

Our Lord Jesus Christ continues to bring joy to all believers, all sinners, and all people of different world religions, because of his great commission for believers. "Go ye therefore, and teach all nations, baptizing them in the name of the Father and of the Son, and of the Holy Ghost: Teaching them to observe all things whatsoever I have commanded you: and, Lo, I am with you always, even to the end of the world." Matt. 28:19- 20.

Christ brings joy to all people in all nations because He does not want anyone to perish; He wants them to gain knowledge of repentance, pray for forgiveness of their sins, and be saved. Jesus Christ still gives us joy today through the power of the Holy Spirit. "I will not leave you comfortless, I will come to you." John 14:18.

"But the Comforter, which is the Holy Ghost, whom the Father will send in my name, he shall teach you all things, and bring all things to your remembrance, whatsoever I have said unto you." John 14:26.

Our Lord said that His Father would send the Holy Spirit, which will abide in the believer forever to teach them and tell them all the things that He wants them to know; he is the *Paraclete* heavenly guest. We believers have joy today because we know that Jesus loves us and that He is coming back to judge the quick and the dead, and all eyes shall see Him.

Therefore, we will continue to have joy no matter what we are going through, day by day; we can still be full of joy because of His love for us. Jesus Christ is the answer to all of the problems of this world.

The true fruit of the Spirit is joy. We must try to exercise joy every day. Many people have looked or are looking for the source of happiness in wrong places everyone on this earth, whether male or female, rich or poor, healthy or unhealthy, or middle class.

Researchers want to know what gives lasting happiness; some of them have thought that if they built the biggest or largest complex mansion, they would be happy, but the result does not last as long as anticipated.

Some people look for happiness in entertainment; they spend millions in entertainment that can sustain them during their mystery, but it is very hard for them to find happiness.

Some look for happiness in athletic hobbies, traveling around the world, dancing, fashion, alcohol, food, and any form of happy hour drugs. None of these forms of happiness enhancement helps them.

For example, King Solomon conducted many experiments with his great wisdom on how to be happy in this world or what can make people happy. King Solomon, at the end of his experimental research, said, "I said in my heart, Go to now, I will prove thee mirth, therefore, enjoy pleasure, and behold, this also is vanity. I said of laughter, it is mad: and of mirth, what does it accomplish?

"I sought in my heart to gratify my flesh with wine, while guiding my heart with wisdom, and how to lay hold on folly, till I might see what was good for the sons of men to do under the heaven all the days of their lives. I made me great work, I build me houses;

"I planted vineyards, gardens, orchards, and planted trees and all many kinds of fruits: King Solomon comes to the awareness and concluded; For God gives to a man that is good in his sight wisdom, and knowledge and joy:

"but to the sinner He gives travail, to gather and to heap up, that He may give to him that is good before

God; This also is vanity and vexation of spirit." Ecc. 2:1-11, 26.

King Solomon realized that only God can determine when He plants the fruit of the Spirit, joy, in our hearts, and whether we experience joy in our lives or not. Seeing people laughing does not mean they are full of joy.

The Bible tells us that everything has a time under the heaven. King Solomon stated that seeing people laugh does not mean they are joyful or experiencing joy. "Even in laughter the heart may ache, and joy may end in grief" Prov. 14:13.

This means that human wisdom is a poor basis for determining what is true or false, what is right or wrong, and what is worthy or unworthy. God's written word of revelation is the only true source for determining the right or wrong path for our lives.

Most of our ways in the system of life lead to death and destruction, but God's way leads to eternal life. King Solomon stated, after his extensive research, that all earthly pleasure, according to his research's findings, are meaningless money, wealth, kingdom of earth, pleasures on earth, cultural activities, delights, no long efforts to find meaningful fulfillment in a good life resulted into true happiness.

He found that he still felt emptiness and had no satisfaction in his life. He realized that we can only find lasting happiness, peace, fulfillment, and joy if we look for our happiness in God's will and in His provisions. King David said, "You will show me the path of life; in your presence is fullness of joy; at your right hand are pleasures forevermore." Psl. 16:11.

As long as we are close to God we will continuously receive incomparable joy that earthly problems cannot destroy. A personal relationship with God gives us confidence and, above all, intimate fellowship and an intimate personal relationship with the Lord's continual presence, bringing His guidance, protection, and joy, with the power of the resurrection and eternal life.

We have to see God's joy as a spring in the desert, flowing to all people—the just and unjust. Experiencing joy is when we get to the point that, through faith, we confidently feel the presence of God in our lives— past, present and future.

"Sing aloud unto God our strength: make a joyful noise unto the God of Jacob." Psl. 81:1. "He should have fed them also with the finest of the wheat: and with honey out of the rock should I have satisfied thee." Psl. 81:16.

When we follow God's orders, He will take total charge of our needs and feed us with the finest foods to eat, and we will experience the real joy and its satisfaction that God provides. God will remove all of our burdens so that we can rejoice in his love.

By then, it will come to us clearly that real joy is our relationship with Him; our relationship with God the Father, through our Lord Jesus Christ, makes this possible through the Lord's teaching of the beatitudes. Matt. 5:1-12.

We must live with joy in order to produce the qualities we need for the kingdom, and our work must produce joy in us as a part of the Holy Spirit's manifestation of God's workmanship through His Spirit.

Biblical joy is inseparable from and incomparable to our relationship with God, which springs down from our knowledge and understanding of the purpose of life and the hope of living with God for eternity when we will enjoy more joy.

If God is truly present in our lives, the joy that God's experience can begin in us will flow through us to other people, "Thou wilt show me the path of life: in thy presence is fullness of joy; at the right hand there are pleasures for evermore." Psl. 16:11.

With eternal pleasure at your right hand, when we experience joy in our lives, it is the sign that shows that our life has found its purpose, and its reason for being alive—it's a revelation of God. Jesus said, "No man can come to me, except the father who hath sent me draw him: and I will raise him up at the last day." John 6:44.

The Father is the one who draws people of all nations to Jesus through the Holy Spirit. God's work of drawing applies to all human souls on earth. This drawing can be rejected. Man himself is helpless; he does not have the strength to come to Jesus unless the Father first begins the work of regeneration in his heart and makes him alive.

Many people on earth do not realize that they are in need of Savior. Jesus' teaching made clear that God the Father is the one whose infinite love has acted in our lives, called us, and spoken to our heart.

For example, during our Lord's earthly ministry He felt sorrow for Jerusalem, "O Jerusalem, Jerusalem, which killest the prophets, and stonest them that are sent unto thee; how often would I have gathered thy children together, as a hen doth gathers her brood under her wings, and ye would not." Luke 13:34.

Our Lord shed tears over Jerusalem's unbelievers. He bore witness to the freedom of human freewill that resisted the grace God and the will of God. Our Lord condemns earthy pleasures. He warns that those who exalt themselves in this life will be put to damnation and shame in the kingdom of heaven.

It clearly shows that the joy of the children of God comes from sources that were not sought by the people of the world. Believers in Jesus Christ find joy through humbleness and joy, which is constantly supplied through the indwelling power of the Holy Spirit.

"Then he said unto them, Go your way, eat the fat, and drink the sweet, and send portions unto them for whom nothing is prepared: for this day is holy unto our Lord: neither be ye sorry; for the joy of the Lord is your strength." Neh. 8:10.

"The fear of the Lord is the beginning of wisdom: and the knowledge of the holy is understanding." Prov. 9:10. There is pleasure and joy in God as He works with His creations. God is a God of joy; it is in His joy that we find our strength. God is a joyful God; He always wanted to share His joy with us.

God is the source of real joy, just as He is the source of love, mercy, and truth. The joy of the Lord powerfully impacts lives. Jesus Christ came to reveal God the Father's joy to us; Jesus Christ is our joy.

"Behold my servant, whom I uphold; mine elect, in whom my soul delighteth; I have put my spirit upon him: he shall bring forth judgment to the Gentiles." Isa. 42:1.

The Messiah was to be one in whom the Father would delight; Jesus Christ was anointed with the oil of Joy. "Thy throne, O' God, is for ever and ever: the scepter of thy kingdom is a right scepter. Thou lovest righteousness, and hatest wickedness: therefore God, thy God, hath anointed thee with the oil of gladness above thy fellows." Psl. 45:6-7.

Our Lord said, "These things have I spoke unto you, that my joy might remain in you, and that your joy might be full." John 15:11. "And now come I to thee; and these things I speak in the world, that they might have my joy fulfilled in themselves." John 17:13.

The declaration of God's Word, accompanied by a sincere desire to follow its instruction, will result in true, heartfelt joy. This Joy of our Lord is based on reconciliation with God, in the presence of the Spirit in our lives. It is maintained by the assurance that we believers have been forgiven in Christ and that we have been restored to fellowship with God and now live in good harmony according to His will.

Joy acts as a fortress to guard us from the troubles and temptations of each day, as power and motivation to persevere in faith until the end of the world. When it comes to life through faith and walking with God, we might want to be in a hurry, but God is never in a hurry because God is never in a hurry.

We are going to try not to grow weary in our journey as He takes us along. We must learn how to appreciate God and how to press on, even when we are feeling tired or weak. God selected pastors, teachers, prophets, apostles, and evangelists to see who are among men and women, and He takes them from among men and women so that they can minister and witness to men and women.

He ministers to these men and women for the benefit of other men and women. We have to learn to differentiate between our happy feelings and cause joy to happen in the heart of God. The joy of the Lord is our strength, because there are going to be times when you are going to be working for God and when you are going to lose your strength. "Rejoice in the Lord always: and again I say, rejoices." Php. 4:4.

124

Believers must rejoice in order to gain strength by recalling all of the great things that the Lord has done for them and through them for other people around them. They must rejoice in the grace of God that abounds more and more in their lives, and also rejoice in the fulfillment of God's promises in their lives and the lives of their children, relatives, and friends.

Believers must always rejoice because joy is one of the important fruits of the Spirit. Joy is our daily bread. We cannot live on the joy we had yesterday; we must have daily joy. Joy gives us strength only when we possess it.

Believers must rejoice and gain strength by recalling the Lord's grace, His full presence in our lives, and His divine promises for us. Joy is an integral part of our salvation in Christ. It is an inner peace and delight in God the Father, the Lord Jesus Christ, and the Holy Spirit, and in the blessing that flows from our relationship with Him.

Joy is associated with the salvation God provides us in Christ and with God's Word. Joy flows from God as one aspect of the Spirit's fruit. It does not come automatically, but is experienced as we maintain an abiding relationship with Christ.

Our joy becomes greater when the Spirit mediates a deep sense of God's presence and nearness in our lives. Our Lord taught us that the fullness of joy is inseparable from and connected to our remaining in

His word, loving others, obeying His commands, and being separate from the world. Joy is delight in God's nearness and in His redemptive gifts.

It cannot be destroyed by pain, suffering, weakness, or difficult circumstances. God the Father made it clear to us that the true joy, the real joy from the heart, lies in the quality of our relationship with him through our Lord Jesus Christ.

Biblical joy is inseparable; our relationship with God, our knowledge, acknowledgement, and understanding of the purpose and hope of heaven with him should shed joy to our minds all the time.

Joy is the sign that our life has experienced God, that God is close to us, and that life has found its purpose for life, through His Spirit, and it also shows that the joy of the children of God is different from the joy of people in the world.

"And they, continuing daily with one accord in the temple, and breaking bread from house, to house, did eat their meat with gladness and singleness of heart." Acts 2:46. "And when he had brought them into his house, he set meat before them, and rejoiced, believing in God with his entire house." Acts 16:34.

The pouring out of the Holy Spirit by Jesus proves that He is the exalted Messiah, the true Son of God, now sitting at the right hand of God and interceding for His believers on earth. He continues to pour out the Spirit on those who believe in Him. The Spirit is Jesus Christ's presence for believers and the Spirit's empowering of believers will continue in their lives as long as they stay close to the Savior and read the Word of God daily.

Even today, when people are first converted they are always full of joy. "And you became followers of us and of the Lord, having received the word in much affliction with joy of the Holy Spirit." 1 Thes. 1:6.

The ultimate source of their joy begins at conversion when they completely give their life to Christ. They receive unspeakable joy. All the words in the chapters of the beatitudes characterize a believer's biblical joy.

In the book of Job, "Knowest thou not this of old, since man was placed upon earth. That the triumphing of the wicked is short, and the joy of the hypocrite but for a moment." Job 20:4-5.

"Folly is joy to him that is destitute of wisdom: but a man of understanding walketh uprightly." Prov. 15:21. When believers in the Lord are filled with the spirit of God, they will feel good about their lives and about who they are, value themselves, and accept themselves for who they are, what they're doing with their lives, where their lives are going, and what they have achieved because of their obedient walking with the Lord.

They will always feel joy and joy will always present in them. Others around them will also notice it.

God is our source of joy; therefore, our relationships with Him are the source and causes of any real, true joy believers might have. "Also that day they offered great sacrifices, and rejoiced, for God had made them rejoice with great joy: the wives also and the children also rejoiced: so that the joy of Jerusalem was heard even afar off." Neh. 12:43.

This was accomplished because they had a good relationship with God. Through the covenant, God himself is the cause and the source of their joy. This should be clear to every believer: that true joy is from God, who is the only producer of joy.

People of this earth can seek joy for their own pleasure but true joy must be sought God's way. True joy comes when people have yielded, surrendered their lives wholeheartedly to the will of God, who makes everything possible in our lives. Joy comes from the fruit of the Holy Spirit; it's rooted in the realization and awareness of God's transforming us into His own image.

Biblical joy arises when people hear the Gospel, review it, understand the grace of God, and believe in salvation with a repentant heart. Hearing and believing the word of the Gospel leads to repentance and a new life in Christ.

"And ye became followers of us, and of the Lord, having received the word in much affliction, with joy of the Holy Ghost." 1 Thes. 1:6.

The Thessalonian believers were going through great stress and confusion due to persecution; yet, in the middle of it, they continued to experience great joy, and their supernatural joy was due to the power of the Holy Spirit working in their lives.

Apostle Paul called it the 'Joy of the Holy Spirit.' Our joy must come from yielding to the fulfillment of God's great creative purpose, accomplished in the lives of all believers. "His Lord said unto him, well done, thou good and faithful servant: thou hast been faithful over a few things, I will make thee ruler over many things: enter thou into the joy of thy lord." Matt. 25:21.

With this word from our Lord, believers must know that their joy does not end here on earth it continues to eternity. "Looking unto Jesus the author and finisher of our faith; who for the joy that was set before him endured the cross, despising the shame, and is set down at the right hand of the throne of God." Heb. 12:2.

"But let those that put their trust in thee rejoice: let them ever shout for joy, because thou defendest them: let them also that love thy name be joyful in thee. For thou, Lord, wilt bless the righteous, with favour wilt thou compass him as with a shield." Psl. 5:11-12.

"For what is our hope, or joy, or crown of rejoicing? Are not even ye in the presence of our Lord Jesus Christ at his coming?" 1 Thes. 2:19.

We believers can always rejoice, knowing that God is always there to help individual believers, just as He continues to help all of the saints scattered around the world.

Apostle Peter, in his Epistle, offers words of encouragement to rejoice so that we can honor God by setting good examples when we are treated badly in the cause of God's services.

Even in times of pain or suffering, believers must continue to rejoice and be happy to participate in the sufferings of Christ our Lord and overjoyed when His glory is revealed.

"Beloved, think it not strange concerning the fiery trial which is to try you, as though some strange thing happened unto you: But rejoice, in as much as ye are partakers of Christ's sufferings; that, when His glory shall be revealed, ye may be glad also with exceeding joy." 1 Pet. 4:12-13.

God, in His plan of salvation, provides an opportunity for everyone living to understand the word of the Gospel, in his or her own language, and to repent and pray for forgiveness, which is only through Jesus Christ.

The Holy Spirit will strengthen us and make us strong, pouring out His patience on us and making us wait patiently with His power. Joy is different than happiness. Joy comes to the heart when a person becomes a believer in Jesus Christ.

The Spirit plants so much joy in the heart of that person that when the believer is going through persecution, affliction, rejection, and all forms of earthly problems and troubles, they will still feel the Holy Spirit's inner joy inside of them.

# 9

# The Fruit of the Spirit: PEACE

We gain contentment through peace in the fruit of the Spirit. "Thou will keep him in a perfect peace, whose mind is stayed on thee because he trusted in thee." Isa. 26:3.

Perfect peace and inward peace lead to fullness of peace with God. Peace of conscience is knowing that one's sins are forgiven when they have asked for it; it is peace at all times and in all circumstances.

God's peace is different than the world's peace. God's peace comes from knowing Him and acknowledging His word; when we allow the Lord to be in control of our lives, our hope of going to heaven is best assured.

Peace does not come from changing circumstances; peace is the result of our personal relationship with the unchanging, all-knowing God of the earth.

The people of the world must first make peace with God almighty, before looking for peace in their lives. Believers will be able to see and know peace of God in all their difficulties and troubles in life.

We can also make peace with everyone around us. Peace of God is perfect contentment of being in the right relationship with God, with others, and with oneself. God is able to use all our difficulties, our circumstances, and our adversities in life for our good and for His glory.

God is the immortal, invisible, and all wise God; He knows what is best and He give the best to his children. He is loving and gracious and will not allow anything to harm us. He is omnipotent, which means there is nothing so great that He cannot solve.

The most important tool for believers is knowing that trusting God is very important in all circumstances of life. The ability to trust God should be demonstrated in the life of believers through willingness to obey God and to follow and do what is right at all times.

Believers must love God and keep His word, abide in Him and His word, and follow Him with peace that surpasses all understanding. The fruit of peace will grow and reach the above; is the peace of God that surpasses all understanding, for our perfect protection, which guards our hearts and minds, so that nothing can harm us beyond what He allows. It is peace beyond any expectation that we cannot imagine.

It is a perfect peace because we are totally connected with Him, to the point that we are at the center of Jesus Christ, the Prince of Peace. His peace fills us and overflows to other people around us. We begin to pour ourselves into other people and become problem-solvers or peacemakers.

Most importantly, we begin to multiply ourselves people learn from us and teach others. The peace follows as the river flows to so many areas of people's lives around us. Peace is the one of the fruits of righteousness.

Peace means an absence of civil disturbance or hostilities, or a personality free from internal and external strife. The biblical concept of peace is larger than anything we can imagine and rests heavily on the peace of God, which means to be complete, to sound good, to be completely whole, or to live well.

The covenant was always renewed or maintained with a peace offering such as prosperity, success, or fulfillment. The people of Israel used peace for greetings and farewells. It was meant to act as a blessing on the one to whom it was spoken.

Believers' lives must be filled with good health, prosperity, and victory. Peace must express completeness and safety. Peace is not a state of mind or a circumstance in nature it is a condition of the heart.

It is a fruit of the Spirit, a gift from God. People must know that true peace consists in the God of peace and in God's peace that sanctifies God's children. God alone is the source of peace, for He is "Yahweh Shalom." The Lord came to sinful humankind, historically, first to the Jews and then to the Gentiles desiring to enter into a relationship with Him.

He established with them a covenant of peace, which was sealed with his presence, "The Lord blesses thee, and keeps thee: The Lord make His face shine upon thee, and is gracious unto thee. The Lord lifts up His countenance upon thee, and gives thee peace." Num. 6:24-26.

The people and the participants were given perfect peace so long as they maintained a proper relationship with the Lord. "Thou wilt keep him in perfect peace, whose mind is stayed on thee: because he trusted in thee. "Isa. 26:3.

"Now the Lord of peace Himself gives you peace always by all means. The Lord be with you all." 2 Thes. 3:16. Throughout the Old Testament and the New Testament, it was anticipated and confirmed that God's peace would be mediated through the Messiah.

Peace with God came through the death and resurrection of Jesus Christ. Peter declared to Cornelius: "The word which God sent unto the children of Israel, preaching peace by Jesus Christ: He is the Lord of all." Acts 10:36.

The Scripture specifically states that there can be no peace for the wicked. Peace could be disturbed if one does not live before the Lord and with each other in righteousness.

"And the God of peace shall bruise Satan under your feet shortly. The grace of our Lord Jesus Christ be with you. Amen." Rom. 16:20. Our heavenly father is the God of peace; our Lord Jesus Christ is the Prince of Peace.

Peace is a condition of a positive nature in which there is active fellowship, harmony, and joy between individuals. Peace is a blessing that ought to be desired and engaged through the peace that God has provided, which allows access through the Spirit to the Father.

All believers belong to the family of God and peace allows us to reside in the temple of the Lord, a habitation of God in the Spirit. Peace comes when we are justified by the loving sacrifice of Jesus Christ's blood and continues to revive God's life.

Peace is with people around us. Peace comes from God and surpasses all understandings. Peace is produced when believers are one with Jesus Christ and blessed with the joy of justification, along with reconciliation, with both God and man.

Peace will come and be produced naturally. In order to maintain peace with God, we have to stay close to the Lord, focus on our Lord, love God's Word, keep His commandments, be diligent in prayer, fill our minds and souls with spiritual thoughts, and be of one mind of passion for one another.

When we have peace with God, we have peace within us whereby we are in a better position to make peace with others. Believers must pursue peace all of the time, have compassion for one another, love our neighbor, and be tenderhearted and courteous.

Believers should not return evil for evil, but rather, respond with a blessing. If we want to bear all fruits scripture says: "And the fruits of righteousness, is sown in peace of them that make peace." Jas. 3:18.

God wants all of us to enter into a true sanctification process with Him so that He can begin the process of molding, shaping, and transforming us into the image of his son Jesus Christ.

He wants to make us into better and holier people, filled with all the fruit of the Holy Spirit. He wants to transform us by renewing our minds. He wants to put correct thinking into our thought process.

Believers must be willing to cooperate with the Holy Spirit, by staying in the word in order to find out what God is going to change in their life, and what God wants to plant in them for them to fully belong to Him. The fruit of the Holy Spirit comes directly from God Himself.

All believers should do the best they can to cooperate and work with the Holy Spirit, allowing all of the fruits to work in our personality. All of these fruits can dramatically change the quality of life and the state of well-being of believers, if they allow the Holy Spirit to work these fruits into their personality. God's joy and God's goodness can become manifest.

Peace derives from remaining in a relationship with God. Peace is tranquility a state of rest that comes from seeking God. Peace is the opposite of violence and chaos. Peace is one of the most important fruits of the Holy Spirit that all the believers in Jesus Christ seek and find.

Peace is what the Spirit of God produces when He dwells in us. When a believer is filled with the peace of God, peace touches everyone around him or her.

The word, peace, expresses an idea of wholeness, completeness, and tranquility in the soul that is unaffected by outward circumstances or pressures. When a believer is dominated by peace, he has a unique character, calmness, and inner stability that results in the ability to conduct himself peacefully everywhere.

Even in the midst of any situation that could be traumatic or upsetting, without allowing the difficulties or pressures of life to break him. A believer who is possessed by peace is a stable person in all that he does.

Jesus Christ is the prophet and Prince of Peace on earth. He brought peace to the hearts of those who made Him the Lord of their lives. Christ said, "Peace I leave with you, my peace I give unto you: not as the world giveth, give I unto you, let not your heart be troubled, neither let it be afraid." John 14:27.

"Therefore being justified by faith, we have peace with God through our Lord Jesus Christ." Rom. 5:1.

"Now the God of hope fill you with all joy and peace in believing, that ye may abound in hope, through the power of the Holy Ghost." Rom. 15:13.

# 10

# The Fruit of the Spirit: PATIENCE

P atience denotes mercy, forbearance, fortitude, patient endurance, and longsuffering. Patient believers have the ability to endure persecution and all sorts of ill treatment from those who hate God.

Patient believers have the power to exercise revenge but decide not to do so. Patience is also known as loyalty, perseverance continuance, bearing up, steadfastness, supportiveness, and hanging on to the promise of God.

Patient endurance means having unshaking faith and having the energy or courage to continue to bear under difficulties, situations, and circumstances, with hope that resists defeat. "For ye have need of patience, that, after ye have done the will of God, ye might receive the promise." Heb. 10:36.

"Strengthened with all might, according to His glorious power, unto all patience and longsuffering with joyfulness." Col. 1:11.

All of the fruits of the Holy Spirit are manifest in our lives; it is the sign that lets us know that we are fully with the Holy Spirit—when people see evidence of its fruit in us. Patience is one of the most important fruits of the Spirit that every believer of Christ must have in order to be able to receive His blessings.

Patience is a self-disciplinary behavior that does not retaliate against people's wrongs. When a believer possesses the fruit of patience, if someone does that believer wrong, he will respond with the Spirit of patience, which is the ability to accept delay or disappointment, take wrongs without getting angry or upset, to continue steadfast under any circumstances, and to continue waiting on the Lord.

Patience is calm endurance based on the certain knowledge that God is in control. Patience helps believers when they are hurting because of a situation over which they don't have control. With the help of the Lord, they may become a source of help, beauty, energy, and healing for those who are sick.

It is very difficult to be patient, because there are many circumstances that make patience contrary to human nature; but, as we get close to the Lord, He produces the fruits of the Spirit patience in us.

Most people in the world are very impatient and, most of the time, very angry. They scream, yell at each other while driving, and when passing each other, most of the time, without knowing what they are yelling about.

Patience is difficult because of the cultural diversities of many people in our society or communities. Patience is contrary to some people's cultures, ethnicities, and lifestyles.

While people in developing, underdeveloped, and Third World countries live simply, in a relaxed and laid back way, people in developed countries are always in a hurry, rushing in and rushing out to things they don't even know and of which they have no knowledge.

They do not understand why people in other countries are so different from them. The Bible says: "He that is slow to wrath is of great understanding: but he that is hasty of spirit exalted folly." Prov. 14:29. "A wrathful man stirreth up strife: but he that is slow to anger appeaseth strife." Prov. 15:18.

We need to develop a character of patience in our lives. The only way that we can develop patience is to abide in Christ; the Holy Spirit will produce patience in us so that we will be able to help others.

As our Lord said in the book of John, we are the branches; if we abide in him, we will bear more and more fruits, and we will receive the best nourishment from Him.

After believers' conversions, they receive eternal life and the power to remain in Christ. With that power, believers must then accept that responsibility in salvation and remain in Christ.

The word, abide, means to live in Christ, just as the branch has life only as long as the life of the vine flows into it, so too believers have Christ's life only as long as Christ's life flows into them through their remaining in Christ.

The conditions by which we remain in Christ are: by keeping God's Word continually in our hearts, maintaining the habit of constant intimate communion with Christ in order to draw strength from Him, obeying His commands, remaining in His love and loving each other, keeping our lives clean and pure through the Word, resisting all sin, and yielding to the Spirit's direction.

We cannot and will not produce unless we abide in Christ; we must stay, read the Word of God daily, walk in His footsteps, pray without cease, spend time with Him in prayer and fellowship, and worship and reflect upon His holiness and what He is doing in our lives.

We need to patiently overlook the many things that bring frustration into our lives. "And Moses said unto the people, Fear ye not, stand still, and see the salvation of the Lord, which he will shew to you today: for the Egyptians whom ye have seen

to day ye shall see them again no more forever."
Exo. 14:13-14.

Therefore, we must be still and wait patiently on
the Lord; our God has the power and energy to han-
dle our problems. "The Lord is not slack concerning
his promise, as some men count slackness; but is longsuffering to usward, not willing that any should perish, but that all should come to repentance." 2 Pet. 3:9.

God is patience and He wants everybody to gain
knowledge of repentance and be saved; everyday, He is
waiting for His creations to come to Him. Our Lord
Jesus Christ opens the door of salvation because of His
patience; the door to our Lord Jesus opens because the
Lord is patient.

The opportunity to be saved from our past and
future sins is still available because the Lord is patient;
He does not want anyone to perish. Rom. 8:25. "But if
we hope for that we see not, then do we with patience
wait for it." Rom. 8:25.

"For they said unto me, make us gods, which
shall go before us: for as for this Moses, the man that
brought us up out of the land of Egypt, we wot not
what is become of him." Exo. 32:23.

When the children of Israel were sitting at the
bottom of Mount Sinai, waiting for Moses to come
down from the mountain, several of them were so
impatient that they went to Aaron to ask him for
another god.

Moses was very angry at their impatience. Patience is one of the most difficult fruits of the Spirit to possess. It is a virtue that Christians, especially teens, wish to possess. God's timing is very important in the lives of believers because God might have other blessings for us, beyond those that we request.

No one can know God's way—we must trust him. If the promise is delayed, he knows the right time for everything in our life. Delayed promises always come with more blessings, and more rewards from the Lord. "The discretion of a man deferreth his anger; and it is his glory to pass over a transgression." Prov. 19:11.

Patience could be described as the willingness to endure disappointment, pain or suffering, without getting angry or giving up. Patience is also attributed to God's slow anger. God is slow to get angry with His people. He is patient with His people, despite the disappointment, pain, and suffering that we cause Him every day.

God is patient with us. God is the same yesterday, today, and forever. He is unchangeable, the God of heaven and earth; He continues to be slow to anger with us. He is full of steadfast love for us. We walk by the Spirit; we live, move, and exist through the Spirit.

We must be thankful to God for His patience, as we express our thankfulness to God, by being patient with our fellow citizens. Patience with one another is the true worship of God. Patience is the fruit of the Spirit; patience is the work of God, committed to building patience and perseverance in the lives of His people.

Patience reflects God in our characters; patience gets us through all circumstances in life and transforms our lives and the lives of the people around us. "Rest in the Lord, and wait patiently for him: fret not thyself because of him who prospereth in his way, because of the man who bringeth wicked devices to pass." Psl. 37:7.

"I waited patiently for the Lord; and he inclined unto me, and heard my cry." Ps. 40:1 "And therefore will the Lord wait, that he may be gracious unto you. And therefore will he be exalted, that he may have mercy upon you: for the Lord is a God of judgment blessed are all they that wait for him." Isa. 30:18.

Waiting patiently for God allows us to see His plan, to work, and to receive the blessings that He prepares for us; while waiting, we are able to be patient with other people around us. We indirectly help them to receive the grace of God in their lives.

Patience is one of the fruits of the Spirit with which everyone, all believers, struggle; it is hard because it takes time to listen, time for our situation to change, and time to wait on Almighty God to move in our lives.

God uses interruptions and trials and, quite often, the people in our lives to develop patience with us.

God stretches us and asks us to deny ourselves and consecrate ourselves to His will. This is the work of our Lord in our lives. He does all this with love and the goal of helping us to become like him so that His will may be fulfilled in our lives and that we may receive His blessings.

God works during the difficult circumstances in our lives in order to produce His character within us, "Knowing this, that the trying of your faith worketh patience. But let patience have her perfect work, that ye may be perfect and entire, wanting nothing." Jas. 1:3-4.

We exercise patience; God wants us to see Him in the middle of all circumstances, conversations, and relationships. "Be still, and know that I am God: I will be exalted among that heathen, I will be exalted in the earth." Psl. 46:10.

"Trust in the Lord with all thine heart, and lean not unto thine own understanding. In all thy ways acknowledge him, and he shall direct thy paths." Prov. 3:5-6.

In patience, we experience quietness and peace. We are able to trust God with what is before us. God is in control; his ways are beyond finding out. He knows what is best for our lives, and He is at work in us. He gave meaning and purpose to our wait.

God wants us to be patient in all circumstances, troubles, afflictions, and tribulations. Being patient is the result of our new life in Christ Jesus. Christ washes us clean from all our sins; Jesus calls us to experience His gift of grace and the newness of life in Him.

We are able to respond to life's circumstances with God's heart, new hearts, new eyes, and the enabling transforming power of the Spirit as part of our new life. "According as his divine power hath given unto us all things that pertain unto life and godliness, through the knowledge of him that hath called us to glory and virtue." 2 Pet 1:3.

"That ye put off concerning the former conversation the old man, which is corrupt according to the deceitful lust; And be renewed in the Spirit of your mind; and that ye put on the new man, which after God is created in righteousness and true holiness." Eph. 4:22-24.

"Therefore if any man be in Christ, he is a new creature: old things are passed away, behold, all things are become new." 2 Cor. 5:17. Believers must fix their eyes, hearts, and minds on Jesus, who gave us a patient hearts; we must trust and rest on His love for us through endurance, longsuffering, and being slow to anger or despair.

"With all lowliness and meekness, with longsuffering, forbearing one another in love; endeavoring to keep the unity of the Spirit in the bond of peace." Eph. 4:2-3.

"But thou hast fully known my doctrine, manner of life, purpose, faith, longsuffering, charity, patience." 2 Tim. 3:10. No human being can create the unity of the Spirit. It already exists for those who believe the truth and have received Christ, just as the apostle proclaimed to all people, not only believers, in Ephesus, that the Ephesians must maintain unity, not through any human efforts or organizations, but by living a life worthy of the calling they had received.

Spiritual unity is maintained by being loyal to the truth and by staying in step with the Spirit—it cannot be achieved by any human efforts. When everything is going our way, patience is easy to practice or demonstrate.

When people treat us unfairly, say bad things about us, or blackmail us, responding with impatience will bring about holy anger, while patience will reveal our faith in God's timing, omnipotence, and love. Most people consider patience to mean passive waiting or gentle tolerance.

Most people wait patiently for the promise of God to be fulfilled in their lives. All believers in Jesus Christ must seek more patience in all areas of life, every day, every moment; we don't want to wait for patience, we don't want to work for it, we want more and more patience to deal with everyday difficulties in life.

In times of war, we need patience to  wait for our loved ones to come back from the battlefield.

Medical doctors and physicians need patience to perform surgery on sick people. Pastors and preachers of the Word of God missionary need patience to witness, pray, preach, and teach for years and yet see little positive response.

All believers need patience when we are at low points in our spiritual lives and do not feel that God is near. Patience is the tool with which Christians' faith holds to the promise of God, even though we may feel much more like the conqueror.

Patience comes from trusting the Lord. Believers exercise patience during the dark events or days in our life; patience helps Christians to not lose hope or control, but rather, to remain firm and steadfast in the conviction that obedience to God is required at all times and in all circumstances.

We must continue to trust when our trust seems to go nowhere, with all our hearts desire; continuing to trust helps us to wait patiently with obedience to our Lord and to continue to be patient. "And Lord passed I by before him, and proclaimed, the Lord, The Lord God, merciful and gracious, longsuffering and abundant in goodness and truth." Exo 34:6.

"The Lord is merciful and gracious, slow to anger, and plenteous in mercy." Psl. 103:8. "The Lord is gracious, and full of compassion, slow to anger, and great mercy." Psl. 145:8.

Our Lord is a God whose compassion, kindness, and forgiveness are united with truth, holiness and justice. The fact that God is gracious and compassionate shows us that He will not punish anyone unless and until His longsuffering love is rejected and despised. "But thou, O Lord, art a God full of compassion, and gracious, longsuffering, and plenteous in mercy and truth." Psl. 86:15.

You are a compassionate and gracious God, slow to anger, abounding in love and faithfulness. Lord, you are gracious and compassionate to all of your children. These repeated words in the Bible express God's delight in showing mercy, especially when He sees misery, which moves His heart to compassion.

He is also slow to become angry at our offenses and quickly shows love and mercy when forgiveness is requested. We must know that all who call on God in truth with sincere and upright hearts must be assured that He is near. He will hear their prayers, fulfill their desires for help, and work for their deliverance.

God's patience or slowness in unleashing His wrath, or anger, is not because of compassion or unwillingness to act; rather, His patient waiting is because he does not wish for anyone to perish, but for all to come to the savior with trust.

The Bible states that all believers must walk in the Spirit, bear one another in love, and show patience to those who are in the world to non-believers as well as the body of Christ. Jesus Christ's desire for the entire body of Christ, His Church, is for us to be joyfully strengthened by Him and to endure this life with patience.

Patience is also known as longsuffering. Longsuffering involves waiting and remaining patient with people who hurt us. We are expected to be patient and correct any wrongdoing and sins with Christ's love. Patience does not mean the same as tolerance.

Tolerance requires people to tolerate or put up with something to accept the issue or situation as agreeable and good even if the person clearly disagrees or if it is prohibited against God's law, or the Word of God. "For ye have need of patience, that after ye have done the will of God, ye might receive the promise." Heb. 10:36.

A patient person is mild, gentle, and constant in all circumstances, no matter what is going on in his or her life; the real test of patience is not in waiting, but in how we behave while waiting during trying circumstances in our lives.

We have a perfect example; the Scriptures tell us that we can be made into a perfect and complete person by having the patience that Jesus showed during his life on earth among us. He was very patient with the scribes and Pharisees.

"Blessed is the man that trusteth in the Lord, whose hope that Lord is. For he shall as a tree planted by the waters, and that spreadeth out her roots by the river, and shall not see when heat cometh, but her leaf shall be green; and shall not be careful in the year of drought, neither shall from yielding fruit." Jer. 17:7-8.

Believers are like a tree planted by water that sends out its roots near the stream. We should not fear when any earthly troubles come or worry about any adversities. We should know that our Lord and Savior is always there for us, to deliver us and sustain us throughout our trials and tribulations.

For example, the prophet Jeremiah was seen as a tree that is close to a stream, whose leaf is always green. We believers are like trees that must be close to a stream in order to bear fruits. Our Lord is the stream; He will provide for His people during hard times and under any circumstances.

We will be able to live for Him and bear more and more fruits to His kingdom. The tree bears the fruit of the Holy Spirit. Christians must produce the fruit of the Spirit, in order to grow and mature spiritually. Blessed are they who keep His words and seek Him with their whole hearts.

The Book of Psalms said, "With my whole heart have I bought have I sought thee, O let me not wonder from the commandments." Psl. 11:10. If we keep His word in our heart at all times, we will be able to understand and follow His commands with our whole heart, be obedient and pray effectively.

The fruits of our heart should be reciprocated with prayers of thankfulness. Our prayers will bring God down to earth and the gates of heaven will open. Our prayers will flow to Heaven if we pray with our whole hearts and with patience.

# 11

# The Fruit of the Spirit: KINDNESS

Kindness is the same as gentleness; it refers to kind behavior towards our neighbors and showing goodness and concern towards them. Sympathetic kindness can also mean showing mercy to others.

Kindness is a gift of the Holy Spirit to us. Kindness is one of the fruits of the Spirit of God that all the believers of Jesus Christ must possess. God wants us to use all of the fruits of the Spirit in our daily lives.

King Solomon, in the Book of Proverbs says, "The desire of a man is his kindness: and a poor man is better that a liar." Prov. 19:22. During his rule as the king of Israel, Solomon was looking for a kind person who had concern for others, who would put the needs of others above his own, who would put the needs of others first, before his own, and who would show kindness to himself and his neighbors. Jesus Christ God the Son is our model of kindness.

He emptied himself because of love when He left His Father's glory in heaven and came to earth. Christ died for our past, present, and future sins on the cross. "Or despisest thou the riches of his goodness and forbearance and longsuffering; not knowing that the goodness of God leadeth thee to repentance?" Rom. 2:4.

God the Father showed great mercy when He sent His one and only begotten Son on earth to redeem us from our sins. Reviewing Christ's kindness should turn you around from being a sinner to a converted Christian.

All believers have received the fruit of the Spirit so that they could exercise it towards their fellow citizens. "Grace be unto you, and peace, from God our Father, and from the Lord Jesus Christ." Php. 1:2.

May the loving kindness of God our Father and the Lord Jesus Christ bless you and give you peace. In summary, kindness is one of the important fruit of the Spirit, which is given to us for the ministerial work, in order to kindly or uniquely minister and witness to people.

When we show people the kindness through the power of the indwelling of the Holy Spirit, people gain tremendous benefits, and we can rejoice that we are using our gift of the Spirit, which is a direct reflection of how close we are and have been to the Spirit of God. If we truly have the gift of the Holy Spirit, we will produce good fruits. "Have mercy upon me, O God, according to thy loving-kindness: according unto the multitude of thy tender mercies blot out my transgression." Psl. 51:1.

King David is an example of kindness, "Wherefore I say unto thee, Her sins, which are many, are forgiven; for she loved much: but to whom little is forgiven, the same loved little." Luke 7:47.

Those who are deeply aware of their own past sinfulness understand how much they have been forgiven and, therefore, they love Jesus very much. Nevertheless, those who have a small understanding of their own sinfulness apart from Christ, will, correspondingly, love him less because they do not comprehend how much they have been forgiven.

Showing kindness is not always easy kindness is difficult. With a concerned, warm, and generous Spirit, however, our Lord Jesus Christ did what He requires. "Saying, Father, if thou be willing, remove this cup from me: nevertheless not my will, but thine, be done." Luke 22:42.

And David said, "Is there yet any that is left of the house of Saul, that I may shew him kindness for Jonathan's sake? and there was of the house of Saul a servant whose name was Ziba.

"And when they had called him unto David, the king said unto him, art thou Ziba? And he said, thy servant is he And the king said, it there not yet any of the house of Saul, that I may shew the kindness of God unto him? And Ziba said unto the king, Jonathan hath yet a son, which is lame on his feet. And the king said unto him, where is he?

"And Ziba said unto the King, behold, he is in the house of Machir, the son of ammiel in lodebar. Then King David sent, and fetched him out of the house of Machir, the son of ammiel, from lodebar. Now when Mehibosheth the son of Jonathan, the son of Saul, was come unto David, he fell on his face, and did reverence.

"And David said, Mephibosheth. And he answered, Behold thy servant. And David said unto him, fear not: for I will surely shew thee kindness for Jonathan thy father's sake, and will restore thee all the land of Saul thy father; and thou shalt eat bread at my table continually.

"And he bowed himself, and said, what is thy servant, that thou shouldest look upon such a dead dog as I am? Then the who is Lame in his feet" so the King said where is he? "Indeed he is in the house of Machir the son of Ammiel, in Lo Deba." Then the King Ziba, Saul's servant, and said unto him, I have given unto thy master's son all that pertained to Saul and to his entire house." 2 Sam. 9:1-13.

Mesphibosheth dwelt in Jerusalem; he ate continually at the king's table for he was lame at both feet. David kept his promise to his close friend Jonathan because he made a covenant with Jonathan before that he would show kindness to his family always. Mephibosheth was the son of Jonathan. David showed this remarkable kindness to him. God wants us to show kindness to others, including our enemies, at all times, in any situation, and in any circumstances.

King Solomon said, "The desire of a man is his kindness: and a poor man is better than a liar." Prov. 19:22. The wisdom of these two men concurs in that kindness is most evident when it is present and, when it is not, its absence is equally evident.

All of the fruits of the Holy Spirit are evident and based on love and kindness, which is the direct manifestation of love from the Holy Spirit. We are full of love because of the Holy Spirit's indwelling power in our hearts; we are full of joy because the Spirit of God will fill us with His joy.

Kindness is conditional behavior towards others; kindness is manifestation of other fruits of the Spirit in our lives, demonstrated by acts of love. Kindness is the work of God that demonstrates the love of God in all areas of our lives and in all instances.

It is very important for all people in this world to show kindness to the people around them. In the book of Second Peter, the Apostle urges us to show brotherly kindness to others. "For if these things be in you, and abound, they make you that ye shall neither be barren nor unfruitful in the knowledge of our Lord Jesus Christ." 2 Pet. 1:8.

Apostle Peter knew that, in order for all believers to grow in all of the fruits of the Spirit, true acknowledgment of brotherly kindness would be needed to seek the heavenly and divine nature, in the world of hatred and violence.

We must accept Jesus and allow His Spirit to live inside of us. In order to show kindness and love to others, we must accept Jesus and allow His divine nature to live through us. We must remember that there is always counterfeit and fake kindness around the world.

Lord Jesus, thank you for your kindness because, while we were yet sinners, you died for our sins. Help us to minister and show kindness as ambassadors, and representatives of your love and kindness on this earth. "Put on therefore, as the elect of God, holy and beloved, bowels of mercies, kindness, humbleness of mind, meekness, longsuffering." Col. 3:12-17.

"And he was withdrawn from them about a stone's cast, and kneels down, and prayed." Luke 22:41. "Wherefore seeing we also are compassed about with so great a cloud of witnesses, let us lay aside every weight, and the sin which doth so easily beset us, and let us run with patience the race that is set before us, Looking unto Jesus the author and finisher of our faith; who for the joy that was set before him endured the cross, despising the shame, and is set down at the right hand of the throne of God." Heb. 12:1-2.

Kindness is an attribute of God and a quality that is desirable but never consistently found in the lives of people in the world. "But love ye your enemies, and do good, and lend, hoping for nothing again; and your reward shall be great, and ye shall be the children of the Highest: for He is kind unto the unthankful and to the evil Be ye therefore merciful, as your Father also is merciful." Luke 6:35-36.

The reward will be great and you will be sons of the Most High, because He is kind to the ungrateful and wicked. The main problem is in understanding kindness and being able to distinguish kindness, mercy, and love. God's kindness is shown in all of his words, beginning in the Garden of Eden when God clothed Adam and Eve with animal skin. God's kindness is manifest in all of his creations.

"The Lord is good to all: and his tender mercies are over all His works." Psl. 145:9. The kindness of God is intended to cause repentance in our lives, not to rejection of Him. We believers in Jesus Christ appreciate God's kindness of forgiveness of our sins, with the blessing of salvation through our Lord Jesus Christ, eternal life, deliverance from fears, afflictions, and troubles.

"If so be ye have tasted that the Lord is gracious." 1 Pet. 2:3. Our salvation derives from the kindness of God. "Wherefore I was made a minister, according to the gift of grace of God given unto me by the effectual working of his power. Unto me, who am less than the least of all saints, is this grace given, that I should preach among the Gentiles the unsearchable riches of Christ." Eph. 2:7-8.

"In order that in the coming ages he might show the incomparable riches of his grace, expressed in his kindness." Eph. 2:7.

It is through of God's continuous kindness that we are saved. "Behold therefore the goodness and severity of God: on them which fell, severity, but toward thee, goodness, if thou continue in his goodness; otherwise thou also shalt be cut off." Rom. 11:22.

If any believer, or Churches of the Lord cut themselves off and followed the false prophets, Paul stated that they would be cut off. This is a serious warning to all people of God, regardless of their denomination, if they do not continue in His kindness, in the apostolic faith, and in the spirit of righteousness.

Kindness and meekness are the same; a kind or meek person is usually seen as a weak person, but a kind person is a very strong person who is the master of himself and a servant to other people.

A kind person will endure and pray instead of revenging wrongs that people do to them. A kind person is never proud; his strength is always under control. Our Lord Jesus Christ is the most kind and meek person on earth. He always exercises His strength under control. When all believers look at kindness, they see clearly that kindness is a condition of the heart and mind, while gentleness describes one's actions.

Kind strength comes from longsuffering and patience, which expresses every situation with love. Believers in the Spirit of kindness are mild, patient, and full of the Spirit of longsuffering. They do not have any Spirit of revenge or retaliation in them. Kind people possess the teachable Spirit and they are able to leave every problem and affliction in the hands of the Lord.

Kindness and meekness, being the fruits of the Spirit, are attributes of God the Father Almighty Himself and are very important to our existing in His image as true witnesses. These characteristics will determine how much peace and contentment are in our lives and how we will perform during our trials. Kindness and meekness are very important.

Our Lord Jesus Christ, in the beatitude, said, "Blessed are the meek" for they shall inherit the earth." Matt. 5:5. Meekness and kindness are active fruits. Both are internal and external in their operation in a believer's life.

When we come to God in deep penitence and with a clear mind of knowledge of ourselves and what God has done, who He is, and what He requires of his people, we will be able to serve God with the Spirit of humility that comes from the Spirit of God. The relationship between humility and kindness is that humility deals with a correct assessment and kindness covers a correct assessment of personal rights.

The example of a meek, kind person is that he or she changes from a selfish, ambitious, and self-willed person who cares about himself or herself alone and who is so proud about who he, to a new man or woman in Christ who has been crucified with Christ.

He or she changes to someone who sees things with the eyes of God or from God's perspective, seeking and focusing only on the Lord, how to serve him, and how to allow and fulfill his purpose in every situation in life. The example of Apostle Paul is that of someone who surrendered all to Jesus.

Paul saw the Father, the Son Jesus Christ, and the Gospel of the kingdom as His main focus; he wanted all the believers to focus their lives on Jesus. Paul told the Corinthian Church that they should imitate him as he imitates Christ. "And be ye kind one to one another, tenderhearted, forgiving one another, even as God for Christ's sake hath forgiven you." Eph. 4:32.

Kindness is the fruit of the Spirit that always acts for the good of other people, regardless of what they do, who they are, or what race or color they are. Kindness will also be seen as goodness and gentleness of heart in any situation with other people.

Kindness is being concerned and acting for the wellbeing of those around us. Kindness is the work of the Holy Spirit in the lives of the believers. Any believer that exercises this type of fruit or the fruit of kindness is considered to be compassionate. Such a person possesses a considerate attitude and is sympathetic to others' needs and problems, kind, gentle, and ready to help people.

The word, kindness, is characterized by interpersonal relationships, which conveys the idea of being an adaptable person to others, someone who can adapt to their problems, situations, and circumstances. A kind person will do good things for people without expecting anything in return.

Kindness is respect and helping others without waiting for someone to help you back. A believer with the fruit of kindness exercises kindness wherever he may be and in any situation. Apostle Paul said, "By pureness, by knowledge, by longsuffering, by kindness, by the Holy Ghost, by love unfeigned, by the word of truth, by the power of God, by the armor of righteousness on the right hand and on the left." 2 Cor. 6:6-7.

Kindness opens doors for serving the Lord. Barnabas, the son of encouragement, sold a field of land and gave the money for the relief of the saints. "Having land, sold it, and brought the money, and laid it at the apostles' feet." Acts 4:37.

Barnabas was very sensitive to hurting people in need of help. The Spirit later marked him as the first fruit. This act of kindness to support the poor was an important part of Barnabas's growth in service of the

Lord, which all the Christians should follow. Kindness softens the hard and angry heart of men. "A soft answer turneth away wrath: but grievous words stir up anger." Prov. 15:1.

Kindness shows Christ to the entire universe. It is with the power of the Holy Spirit that believers are able to produce genuine kindness, and it can only happen once we submit and obey the Holy Spirit, which means totally surrendering to the Holy Spirit's control.

The Spirit nurtures the positive character changes that are reflected in our relationship with the Lord. Through the love of God in our hearts, the Spirit of God is able to produce the fruit of kindness in our lives. Through the love of God, we found the sustaining power of the Holy Spirit, who turned us from unkind persons, to kind persons.

Our heavenly Father continuously pours His love upon all His children. The kingdom of God is righteousness, peace, and joy in the Holy Ghost, and righteousness is its first principle. Its peace-loving and selfless citizens are at war with unrighteousness in all forms.

It is the peace of mind and heart that the captive sinner experiences when He is reconciled with God. We must know that believers who produce the fruit of the Spirit do not come to terms with the unfruitful works of darkness. There is no other person in this world that is sinless like Jesus. He is the one that took away the sin of the whole world through His infinite love for mankind.

We are commissioned to go throughout the earth to tell, teach, and explain the good news of the Gospel, the work of redemption that was completed through Jesus Christ. Christ will return when our obedience with His great commission is fulfilled, so let us obey and go to the ends of the earth for Christ, who is our joy, our peace, and our righteousness.

# 12

# The Fruit of the Spirit: GOODNESS

Goodness is the state or quality of being good, moral excellence, kind feelings, kindness, generosity, the best part of anything, and strength; it is a character recognized in the quality or conduct of a fully Spirit-filled believer.

"Wherefore also we pray always for you, that our God would count you worthy of this calling, and fulfill all the good pleasure of his goodness, and the work of faith with power." 2 Thes. 1:11. "For the fruit of the Spirit is in all goodness and righteousness and truth." Eph. 5:9.

Christians are exhorted to do good works, such as teaching and preaching the Word of God, encouraging, and serving in various ways within the fellowship of believers. "And let us not be weary in well doing: For in due season we shall reap, if we faint not. As we have therefore, opportunity, let us do good unto all men, especially unto them who are of the household of faith." Gal. 6:9-10.

Goodness is a quality that imitates God; when believers are filled with the Holy Spirit, they can exercise the goodness of God through a rich expression that will shows a Christian and Christ like character and a Christian personality.

Goodness and kindness are similar in their emphasis on moral values with a genuine excellence that is worthy of admiration. "A good man out of the good treasure of his heart bringeth forth that which is good: and an evil man out of the evil treasure of his heart bringeth forth that which is evil, for of the abundance of the heart his mouth speaketh." Luke 6:45.

Believers must imitate Christ's goodness to prove that the fruit of the Spirit called Goodness is in our lives; it must be seen in our thoughtfulness, truthfulness, sympathy, fairness, unselfishness, helpfulness, generosity, tolerance, and forgiveness.

If we exercise all these fruits, they will be manifest in our actions in life. God's Words are the source from which we are thoroughly furnished. In all good works, we are directed by the indwelling of the Holy Spirit. "Be not overcome of evil, but overcome evil with good." Rom. 12:21.

God's goodness is the truth of the Scripture. His goodness is praised in the Book of Psalms. Our Lord

Jesus Christ affirms the Father's goodness when speaking to the rich young ruler, "And He said unto him, why callest thou me good none good but one, that is, God: but if thou wilt enter into life, keep the commandments." Matt. 19:17.

"O taste and see that the Lord is good blessed is the man that trusted in Him." Psl. 34:8. God's goodness appears clearly in His dealing with all of His creations; God is not only good to all His created beings, but also to you and me. "Surely goodness and mercy shall follow me all the days of my life: and I will dwell in the house of the Lord forever."

Psl. 23:6. Believers' goodness is structured on divine goodness; goodness involves upright character, which expresses itself in kindness and other praiseworthy qualifications, including avoiding any evil thoughts that spring from the inner being. Goodness always involves particular way of behaving.

God is good. He is good to His people; when people are good they behave decently toward each other, based on God's goodness to them. The biblical words for goodness include the idea of upright behavior. Believers' goodness shows itself in various moral qualities.

Goodness involves not only correct behavior, but also avoiding its opposite, evil. The choice between good and evil has been laid before human beings since the garden of Eden, when Adam and Eve ate the fruit from the tree: "And out of the ground made the Lord God to grow every tree that is pleasant to the sight, and good for food, the tree of life also in the midst of the garden, and the tree of knowledge of good and evil." Gen. 2:9.

Believers who bear the fruit of goodness know that it has never been solely a matter of outward behavior it comes from within. A good person has good behavior, exhibits good behavior, and exhibits a good heart. Old Testament Scripture says that God's goodness to his people and their Goodness in response are based on the covenant between them. Goodness in the New Testament is the fruit of the Spirit.

The tree of the knowledge of good and evil was designed to test Adam's faith and obedience to God and His word. God created humans as moral beings with the ability to choose freely to love and obey their creator, or to disobey him and rebel against His will.

Goodness and love for the Lord will follow Christ's people all the days of their lives, and they surely will dwell in the house of the Lord from now to eternity. The Good Shepherd will accompany believers through life's pilgrimage; they will receive constant, abundant grace to help bring them kindness and support.

No matter what the circumstances are, they can trust the Good Shepherd to work, in all things, for their good. The goal of all believers following the

Good Shepherd and experiencing His goodness and love is that, one day, they will be with the Lord forever and serve him forever in His house.

We are commanded to overcome evil done to us by doing good in return. All Christians must know that it is their responsibility to yield to the Holy Spirit. It is very important that all Christians make the fruit of the Spirit part of their lives.

Yielding one's life to the direction of the Holy Spirit means involving oneself with the Word of God and being a doer of the Word of God not a hearer alone. Christian life is always a combination of the work of the Holy Spirit, God's originating fruit, and the cooperation of the will of God with individual believers of Christ.

Goodness builds up and promotes wholeness; when we focus on the goodness of the Lord, hope, encouragement, and faith are shown in us and we see the best in others and open up to them. We are willing to work together in order to achieve great victory in the goals we set for ourselves.

Believers remain focused on the goodness of God and His call to our lives. We find a deep sense of fulfillment, purpose, and satisfaction. This will change how we approach many things and the way we speak about them.

The Spirit of God will empower us, direct us, and help us to understand the reason why our enemies want to hurt us, by opening our heart to forgive them and showing goodness to those who hurt us. Those who manifest God's goodness think good thoughts, speak good words, and do good deeds.

Their words match what they do, and they maintain consistency of integrity in their lives. Goodness is the state or quality of being good, moral excellence, kind feelings, kindness, generosity, the best part of anything, and strength; it is a character recognized in the quality or conduct of a fully Spirit filled believer.

"Therefore also we pray always for you, that our God would count you worthy of his calling and fulfill all the good pleasure of his goodness, and the work of faith with power." 2 Thes. 1:11. "For the fruit of the Spirit is in all goodness and righteousness and truth." Eph. 5:9.

Christians are exhorted to do good works, such as teaching and preaching the Word of God, and encouraging and serving in various ways within the fellowship of believers. Believers should not be weary in doing good, because the reward will come from Him in due time; they shall reap if they do not lose hope.

Therefore, as we have the ability and the opportunity, let us do good to all, especially to those who are Christians to the entire household of faith. Goodness is a quality that imitates God. When believers are filled with the Holy Spirit, they can exercise the goodness of God through a rich expression that will shows a Christian and Christ like character and a Christian personality.

Goodness and kindness are similar in their emphasis on moral values with a genuine excellence that is worthy of admiration. All believers in Christ always bring out good treasure from their hearts in order to help others.

Believers must imitate Christ's goodness. In order to prove that the fruit of the Spirit, Goodness, is in our lives, it must also be seen in our thoughtfulness, truthfulness, sympathy, fairness, unselfishness, helpfulness, generosity, tolerance, and forgiveness.

If we exercise all of these fruits, they will be manifest in our actions in life. God's Words are the source from which we are thoroughly furnished. In all good works, we are directed by the indwelling of the Holy Spirit. "Be not overcome of evil, but overcome evil with good." Rom. 12:21

God's goodness is a truth of the Scripture. His goodness is praised in the Book of Psalms. Our Lord Jesus Christ affirms the Father's goodness when speaking to the rich young ruler. God's goodness appears clearly in his dealing with all of his creations.

God is not only good to all of His created beings but also to you and me. Believers' goodness is structured on divine goodness; goodness involves upright character, which expresses itself in kindness and other praiseworthy qualifications, including avoiding any evil thoughts that spring from the inner being. Goodness always involves a particular way of behaving.

God is good. He is good to His people; when people are good they behave decently toward each other, based on God's goodness to them. The biblical words for goodness include the idea of correct behavior. Believers' goodness shows itself in various moral qualities. Goodness involves not only correct behavior, but also avoiding its opposite, evil.

The choice between good and evil has been laid before human beings since the Garden of Eden, when Adam and Eve ate the fruit from the tree. Believers who bear the fruit of goodness know that it has never been solely a matter of outward behavior it comes from within.

A good person has good behavior, exhibits good behavior, and exhibits a good heart. Old Testament Scripture says that God's goodness to his people and their Goodness in response are based on the covenant between them. Goodness in the New Testament is the fruit of the Spirit.

The tree of the knowledge of good and evil was designed to test Adam's faith and obedience to God and His word. God created humans as moral beings with the ability to choose freely to love and obey their creator, or to disobey him and rebel against His will.

"Surely goodness and love will follow me all the days of my life, and I will dwell in the house of the

Lord forever." Psl. 23:6. The Good Shepherd will accompany believers through life's pilgrimage; they will receive constant, abundant grace to help bring them kindness and support.

No matter what the circumstances are, they can trust the Good Shepherd to work in all things for their good. The goal of all believers following the Good Shepherd and experiencing His goodness and love is that, one day, they will be with the Lord forever and serve him forever in His house.

We are commanded to overcome evil done to us by doing good in return. All Christians must know that it is their responsibility to yield to the Holy Spirit. It is very important that all Christians make the fruit of the Spirit part of their lives.

Yielding one's life to the direction of the Holy Spirit means involving oneself with the Word of God and being a doer of the Word of God not a hearer alone. Christian life is always a combination of the work of the Holy Spirit, God's originating fruit, and the cooperation of the will of God with individual believers of Christ.

Goodness builds up and promotes wholeness; when we focus on the goodness of the Lord, hope, encouragement, and faith are shown in us and we see the best in others and open up to them. We are willing to work together in order to achieve great victory in the goals we set for ourselves. Believers remain focused on the goodness of God and His call to our lives. We find a deep sense of fulfillment, purpose, and satisfaction. This will change how we approach many things and the way we speak about them.

The Spirit of God will empower us, direct us, and help us to understand the reason why our enemies want to hurt us, by opening our heart to forgive them and showing goodness to those who hurt us.

Those who manifest God's goodness think good thoughts, speak good words, and do good deeds. Their words match what they do, and they maintain consistency of integrity in their lives.

# Summary

Complete, full knowledge and inspiration of the entire Bible is equally God-given from Genesis through Revelation. The Word of God, through Biblical inerrancy, points to the doctrinal position that the Bible is accurate and totally free of error, that Scripture in its original manuscripts does not affirm anything that is not true, or that is an error not only with regards to doctrine, but also with regards to history, science, chronology, and in all other areas of life.

The doctrine of Trinity is considered as being at the center of Christian doctrine. God reveals Himself to humanity through so many of the things that He has created, in such a way that all of His creations may find their meaning in relation to God.

The Spirit Power assists all Christians, including students and scholars of theology, who are interested in understanding their Christians life, in their hearts and minds. This book will be a great resource and a treasure. This book will help all Christians and theology students of all denominations, as well as all people of the other religions, to open up the Scripture for a greater spiritual understanding of the

Spirit Power and open them to the things of God, His power, and His will for all people on earth. The Power of the Holy Spirit in the lives of all believers in the body of Christ on this earth cannot be compared to any power.

It is incomparable, it is immeasurable beyond what anyone can think or imagine. Our Lord said, "But the hour cometh, and now is, when the true worshippers shall worship the Father in Spirit and in truth: for the Father seeketh such to worship Him." John 4:23.

Jesus Christ expounded upon this clearly to the Samaritan woman at the well. We must come to God with sincere hearts and with the Spirit of holiness, leading lives that are under the control of the Holy Spirit; we are created in the image of God.

Our new birth is different from our old birth, which was of the flesh. God's relationship with all of His children is based on the Spirit not on the flesh. It is like the relationship of a Father and His children it can never be erased. We are one in Him as He is one with the Father.

We must worship the Father according to the truth of the Father that was revealed by the Son and that the Holy Spirit controls and guides. The relationship that God requires of us must be a voluntary one that we enter into willingly and joyfully, surrendering our will to the will of God.

Our relationship must remain unconditional and be based on our faith in Christ, throughout our life on earth. Faith demonstrates and is characterized by sincere love and obedience to God. The only true worship is when we worship the Father through the Spirit of Holiness.

God gave us His Spirit and He continues to pour out His Spirit on all those who believe in Him, up until today. Every day, there is always a day of Pentecost in heaven, whereby the Spirit of God pours down into the hearts, minds, and souls of His converted sinners.

God gave us the power of the Spirit to dwell and perform His supernatural power through us, so that we may be able to live lives originating in the Lord here on earth. I urge all members of the body of Christ to use this power, claim this power, and use it in everywhere, in everything they do. He is waiting for you and me.

There is no power but the power of the Spirit of God in our lives, in the lives of our children, relatives and friends. Use the power of the Spirit of God in your office, neighborhood, community, city, state, and in the entire world with the unending love of the Spirit that dwells in you.

Exercise all the fruit of the Spirit wherever you go: love, joy, peace, goodness, kindness, and the other fruits of the Spirit. Allow the Spirit of God to continuously produce and pour out the fruits of His Spirit in our lives.

The Spirit of God the Father, the Spirit of God the Son, and the Spirit of God the Holy Spirit is one, and He made us one in Him. We should rejoice and continue in unending love and in the Spirit Power.

Jesus Christ is the truth; all believers must live in unity and speak the truth that Christ requires of us. Those who do not have the truth in them hide what is in their heart and they remain in darkness and automatically throw themselves outside the kingdom of heaven. Believers must speak the truth with the love of God.

# Bibliography

Walter A. Walter Editor Evangelical Dictionary of Biblical Dictionary of Biblical Theology: Publisher Baker Book House, Grand Rapids, MI, USA.

William MacDonald, Edited by Art Farstad: Believer's Bible Commentary, Thomas Nelson Publisher, Nashville, TN, USA.

Thomas F. Torrance, Paul D. Molnar 1946. Ashgate publisher, Ltd: Distributed by Syndetic Solutions, Inc. Theologian of the Trinity. Christian Denominations Doctrine Theology the Bible. Farnham, England, Burlington, VT, USA.

Mathew Henry's Commentary in one Volume, Edited by Re. Leslie F. Church: Zondervan Publishing House, Grand Rapids, MI, USA.

D. Norman Geisler: Systematic Theology Volume Four, Church Last Thing, Bethany House Publishers, Bloomington, MN, USA.

Leadership Ministries Worldwide: Practical Word Studies in the New Testament Volume One and Volume Two from the Publishers of The Preacher's Outline and Sermon Bible: Zondervan Publishing House, Chattanooga, TN, USA.

James D. Smart: The Interpretation of Scripture, the Westminster Press, Philadelphia, PA, USA.

# Biblical Index

Ecclesiastes: 2:1-11, 26

Isaiah: 4:4, 55:8-9, 65:3, 42:1, 26:3, 30:18, 25:1, 53:7-9

Jeremiah: 15:15, 29::11, 17:7-8

Ezekiel: 36:26-27, 37:3-5

Hosea: 10:12, 2:20

Joel: 2:13, 2:28-32

Zechariah: 4:6

Matthew: 28:19-20, 5:1-12, 25:21, 9:17, 19:17, 11:23-24, 6:4, 6, 11:29, 5:5-6, 9:3-6, 18:23-35, 8:4, 9:3-6, 18:23-35 8:4, 5:6, 6:33 11:11

Mark: 16:16

Luke: 23:34, 1:35, 2:10-11, 13:34, 6:35-36, 6:45, 11:13, 7:47, 22:4, 6:45, 16:10-12, 18:7, 9:48, 9:48, 3:8, 19:23

John: 4:24, 1:3, 1:1, 4:23-24, 14:7-9, 15:1-2, 14:16, 26, 16:8, 16:13, 16:7-8, 3:6, 6:63, 4:14, 7:37-38, 3:3-8, 86:16, 4:23-24, 15:10, 13:35, 4:7-8, 3:16, 15:13, 4:19, 1:11, 6:44, 17:13, 15:11, 14:27, 12:27, 16:13, 13:17, 1:7-9, 20:24-31, 3:3, 20:26, 16:22, 20:21, 16, 12-14, 20:21, 16:21, 4:23, 14:6, 16:13, 6:12, 2:25, 13:1

Acts: 11:16-17, 2:3-4, 2:38, 8:14-15, 3:31, 24:24-25, 9:17, 10:44, 1:8, 1:4, 5:31, 16:30, 12:46, 16:34, 16:24-25, 10:36, 8:35-38

Romans: 8:16, 8:16-17, 6:3-4, 8:15-16, 8:27, 1:29-31, 13:13, 5:5, 8:14, 16:20, 8:25, 2:4, 11:22, 5:8, 8:11, 5:1, 15:13, 12:21, 10:17, 7:14-17, 8:3-4, 2:4, 9:22-24, 15:1-2, 10:10, 2:4, 3:25, 12:3

1 Corinthians: 10:31, 6:6-10, 13:1-13, 8:1, 13:4-8, 2:13-14, 13:13, 13:4-8, 1:1110:13, 9:27

2 Corinthians: 5:19, 5:17, 5:5, 3:18, 12:20, 12:9-10, 6:6-7, 1:18-19, 8:9, 10:1, 5:17, 12:7

Galatians: 5:22, 5:19-23, 5:18, 6:9-10, 5:23, 2:20, 6:1

Ephesians: 1:13-14, 1:13-14, 2:1-3, 5:2, 1:20, 4:22-24, 4:2-3, 2:7-8, 4:32, 5:5-9, 3:16-17, 2:8, 4:2, 3:16, 5:17-25, 1:17

Philippians: 4:8, 2:7-8, 2:13, 4:4, 1:2, 3:9, 5:11, 2:5-8, 3:10

Colossians: 1:15-16, 3:12-17, 4:7, 1:7, 1:16, 15:1,8,16, 3:13, 3:12-15

1 Thessalonians: 1:6, 4:16-17, 3:16, 1:11, 2:23-26

2 Thessalonians: 1:6, 2:7-8, 1:6

2 Timothy: 3:10, 2:24, 2:25

Titus: 3:5, 3:2-3

Hebrews: 12:3, 12:2, 12:1-2, 11:6, 1:1-2, 12:2, 10:36, 11:6

James: 3:18, 1:3-4, 1:21, 1:5, 3:171

1 Peter: 5:7, 4:12-13, 2:3, 3:4, 3:18, 3:18-20, 3:15, 3:14 5:5-6

2 Peter: 3:9, 1:3, 1:5-11, 1:5-7, 3:9

1 John: 4:9, 4:4, 3:1, 4:7-12, 4:16, 2:3-6

Revelation: 21:3

# Benediction

66 The grace of our Lord Jesus Christ, the love
of God, and the communion of the Holy
Ghost, be with you all." Amen, amen, amen.
2 Cor. 13:14.

MAY GOD BE GLORIFIED FOR THE GREAT
THINGS HE HAS DONE IN OUR WORLD.

Books previously
published by the author
Grace Dola Balogun by
Grace Religious Books Publishing
& Distributors, Inc.

**PRAYER THE SOURCE OF STRENGTH**
**FOR LIFE – English Edition**

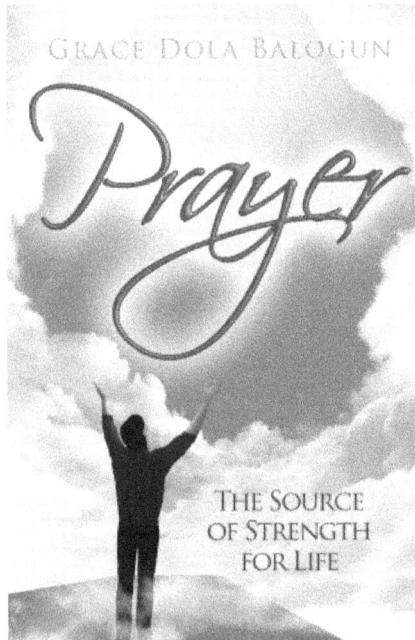

*Prayer the Source of Strength for Life* is a powerful book that will energize your spirit to pray more and more until the prayer is part of your life and until the gate of heaven is opened and your prayer is answered. Your prayer life will change your life.

## LA ORACION FUENTE DE FORTALEZA PARA LA VIDA – Spanish Edition.

Dios nos dio el poder de la oracion, quiere que lo usemos; debemos illamar, comunicarnos con el en todo lo que estemos pasando. El espera saber de nosotros.

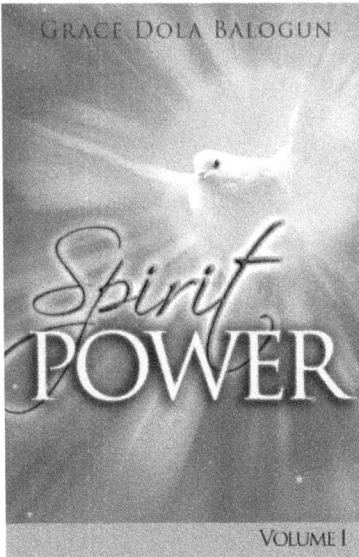

*Spirit Power Volume I and II* both discuss the power of the Holy Spirit in the life of believers of Jesus Christ.

The Power of the Spirit of God begins from the creation of the world up until today. That power will also continue until Christ returns to reign. Hallelujah!

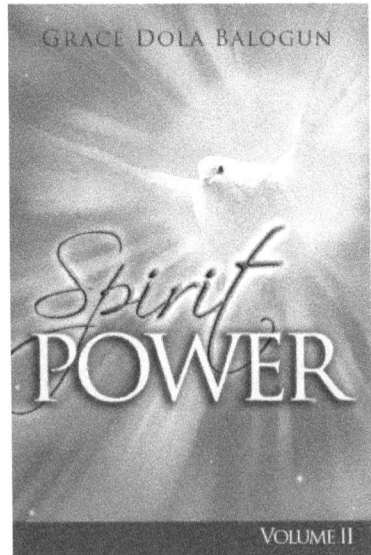

# THE CROSS AND THE CRUCIFIXION

Our Lord Jesus Christ died on the Cross to bring forth love and compassion. Sin's impact on human life brings all other evil into our world, from one society to another society, from one culture to another.

But in Christ, we are clothed with His holiness. We have the gift of eternal life. The gate of heaven is open and we are eligible for our inheritance in heaven.

Hallelujah! Hosanna in the Highest. Jesus Christ paid it all, unto Him all we owe. The Cross of Christ is the Cross of joy, peace, and righteousness to all who believe in Him.

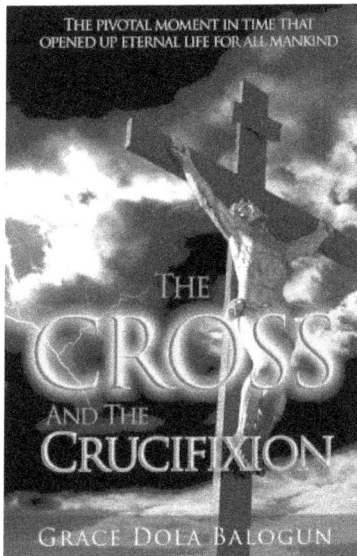

THE PIVOTAL MOMENT IN TIME THAT OPENED UP ETERNAL LIFE FOR ALL MANKIND

THE CROSS AND THE CRUCIFIXION

GRACE DOLA BALOGUN

# About the Author

Grace Dola Balogun graduated from Fordham University Graduate School of Religion and Religious Education in the year 2010 with an M.A. in Religion and Religious Education. She has been a prayer mentor and advisor for many Christians of all denominations since 1988.

Visit her online at:
gracereligiousbookspublishers.com
Prayerstrengthforlife.com
Spiritpower.info
salvationcompleted.com
Facebook
GSTwitter@prayersource

# To Order This Book

To order additional copies of this book,
please E-mail:
info@gracereligiousbookspublishers.com

This book may also be ordered from 30,000
wholesalers, retailers, and booksellers in
the U. S., and in Canada and over
100 countries globally.

To contact Grace Dola Balogun for an
interview or a speaking engagement,
please E-mail:
info@gracereligiousbookspublishers.com

The Spirit and the bride say, "Come!"
And let the one who hears say, "Come!"
Let the one who is thirsty come;
and let the one who wishes take
the free gift of the water of life.

Revelation 22:17

*MARANATHA!*

*COME, LORD JESUS!*

* 9 7 8 0 9 8 5 1 4 6 0 7 8 *